RICHMOND COLLEGE, 1843-1943

RICHMOND COLLEGE
1843-1943

EDITED BY
FRANK H. CUMBERS
(Richmond 1927–31)

WITH FOREWORDS BY
LESLIE F. CHURCH
(Resident Tutor 1929–35)
AND
ERIC S. WATERHOUSE
(Richmond 1898–1901: Principal 1940–   )

WIPF & STOCK · Eugene, Oregon

Wipf and Stock Publishers
199 W 8th Ave, Suite 3
Eugene, OR 97401

Richmond College 1843-1943
By Cumbers, Frank H. and Church, Leslie F.
Copyright©1944 Methodist Publishing - Epworth Press
ISBN 13: 978-1-5326-3822-0
Publication date 7/27/2017
Previously published by Epworth Press, 1944

Every effort has been made to trace the current copyright
owner of this publication but without success. If you have
any information or interest in the copyright, please contact the publishers.

CONTENTS

PREFACE		7
FOREWORD	*Leslie F. Church*	8
'ALMA MATER'	*Reginald Glanville*	9
FOREWORD	*E. S. Waterhouse*	11
PROLOGUE		13

Part One
The Spirit of Richmond

RICHMOND AND 'THE FIELD'	*Reginald Glanville*	17
RICHMOND AND EVANGELISM	*W. E. Sangster*	24
RICHMOND AND THE FUTURE	*Kenneth Underwood*	30

Part Two
The Place

THE STORY OF RICHMOND	*Frank Cumbers*	35
THE TREASURES OF RICHMOND		
1. THE RICHMOND WESLEYANA	*C. Ryder Smith*	52
2. THE COLLEGE PORTRAITS	*S. G. Dimond*	54

Part Three
Down the Years

SIXTY YEARS AGO	*A. J. Norman and W. H. Hart*	61
A RICHMOND 'LOG'	*George Jackson*	68
FIFTY YEARS AGO	*E. Stanley Edwards*	74
FORTY YEARS AGO	*Arthur Walters*	77
THIRTY YEARS AGO	*Leslie D. Weatherhead*	81
TWENTY YEARS AGO	*Frank B. Roberts*	88
A TUTOR'S MEMORIES	*Thos. H. Barratt*	94

Part Four
The Tutors and the Studies

THE TUTORS . . . . . *Frank Cumbers* 99
STUDIES—AND STUDENTS . . . *E. S. Waterhouse* 123

Part Five
The Men

THE MEN OF RICHMOND 128
E. J. Ives, Wilfrid Hannam, and Frank Cumbers
MEMBERS ONE OF ANOTHER . . *Frank Cumbers* 146

EPILOGUE 156

Records

CHRONOLOGICAL LIST OF TUTORS 159
TABLE OF SENIORITY 161
COLLEGE OFFICIALS 162
CHRONOLOGICAL LIST OF MEN 163

INDEX 189

PREFACE

'To no man living is it given to write the history of Richmond College.' In this fashion Mr. T. H. Barratt begins his essay; and nobody can be more conscious of this than I: This book represents the effort, and presents the joyous and grateful memories of many Richmond men who have talked together, written to their fellows, and finally offered this tribute to 'Richmond, our Mother'. I speak for them all in saying that no work will ever be more a labour of love.

It will be obvious that I have drawn on Mr. Brash's *Story of the Colleges* and on Dr. Barber's *Short History of Richmond*, and my thanks are due to them, and also to the compilers of *The Richmond Traditions* (see p. 31), to Mrs. W. A. Kirkham for the cover design, to D. M. Rowlands for the cartoon facing p. 150, and to G. N. Stephens for the poem on p. 20; to Kenneth Underwood, Secretary, 1940; to the Editor of the *Methodist Recorder* and his staff for very kind help, and to the Book-Room Staff, especially Mr. R. W. Young of the Editorial Department.

I am very deeply indebted to Dr. Ryder Smith and Dr. Waterhouse for constant and unstinted guidance and help, and I would thank my wife for a careful, critical reading of the typescript and for many suggestions, and Miss Sylvia Gibbs for much help in typing and with the Records. The following have also greatly helped with suggestions and details: G. Kellett Grice, James Lewis, Franklyn G. Smith, Thos. Stephenson, R. R. Tregunna, Spencer Watkins, George R. Forde (South African details), H. L. Bishop (the French work), and many others.

Generally speaking, degrees and prefixes of all kinds have been omitted in the case of those who belong to the family. Finally, the Editor is not responsible for opinions expressed in any contributions except his own.

FOREWORD

I AM a Headingley man—but a Headingley man tinged with Richmond. It is an unspeakable privilege to have known the fellowship of both Colleges.

This book has helped me to remember many things. Amongst all the memories the most vivid is not that of fires or escapades, or even the burden of Mana—it is the silence of early Communion in the little Chapel in the tower. Nothing can erase the recollection of those Saturday mornings. They will bind me for ever to all Richmond men, for together we shared the mystery of the Presence and accepted anew our divine commission. Beyond the ends of the earth this memory will go with us. Past the reckoning of Time we shall remember.

Whenever we meet, because of this sacred bond, we shall cry out with joy 'All hail!' and when we part we shall say—as the old translator put it—'Well fare thee'. And so, to Richmond past, present—yes, and to Richmond to be—we say: 'God bless you, that you may bless.'

LESLIE F. CHURCH

ALMA MATER

WHAT shall we say of her—
Richmond, our Mother?
How shall we speak of her?
Silent herself?
How, with assoiled lips
Translate her spirit pure,
Strike you her image here,
Richmond, our Mother?

Heart of all constancy,
Arms of devotion,
Mother of manliness
Kindly and strong;
God's breath her Talisman,
God's work her labour here,
Christ's love her motive true,
Richmond, our Mother.

Well has she nursed her sons,
Nor feared their travail,
Wrought for their weaning from
Weakness and self;
Sent them to many climes,
Given them for others' woes,
Bid them oft think of her,
Richmond, our Mother.

Born of no human will,
In heaven her parentage,
Dear and adorable
Daughter of God!
Age cannot spoil her grace,
Time cannot steal her strength,
Sons are her only care,
Richmond, our Mother.

What shall we say of her,
Who are her children?
How shall we speak of her,
Silent herself?
How, save by loving her,
Manfully serving her,
Being true sons to her,
Richmond, our Mother?

REGINALD GLANVILLE, 1922–5.

Tune, 'Loyalty', by R. W. Debenham Peck, 1928–31.

FOREWORD

SEPTEMBER 15, 1843. The young Queen was on the throne, and her Prime Minister, Peel, was facing the 'hungry forties' and the Corn Laws. The literary world was talking about the two-volume edition of the poems of the young man Tennyson, contrasting his golden phrasing with the 'uncouth' Browning. Carlyle was at the height of his powers. But London Methodists were minded of other things. Was it not on this day that the new 'Institution' should be opened at Richmond in Surrey?

Methodism's first effort at a college for training the ministry had been at Hoxton in 1835, to which was added later Abney House, Stoke Newington. Finally, it was decided that there should be a new Institution House in the London area, and 'a second' in the neighbourhood of Manchester. Actually it was found easier to get a site near Manchester than near London, so Didsbury was completed a year earlier than Richmond.

On this ground, Didsburians vainly talk of the priority of their college! No Richmond man is deceived by the speciousness of this claim, based on the accident of building! Richmond is the direct successor of the London college. That this was the view taken at the time is indicated by the elusive and scurrilous 'Fly Sheets' (1844). Attacking Dr. Bunting, the President of the Institution, the anonymous author remarks: 'A branch, it is true, has been established at Didsbury, but still the parent expects to have homage rendered to it in the Metropolis.' Richmond concedes that Didsbury is the older building, but claims to be, none the less, the 'parent' college.

One cannot help wondering what the old students would have thought had they returned on the Centenary Day. Outside, the building is much the same, save for an extra story added to the wings. Some of the fine old trees would still have greeted them—the deciduous cypress, the fir, acacia, weeping ash and the famous mulberry tree. Had they gone within they would have seen great differences. The famous statue of John Wesley still stands in the hall to greet every neophyte in his band of 'travelling preachers', but the beautiful new Library, standing where another generation played rackets, the new main stairway, the games-room, common-room, the dressing, changing, and bath-rooms, the bedrooms with hot and cold water! Cleanliness may have been next to godliness even in 1843, but there was reserved a much larger place for the latter than for the former! The older generation, whiskered and bearded even in their twenties, shown in the college photographs standing stiffly with their white choker ties and frock-coats, would deem their successors to be youths, callow and unshaped, in comparison.

The old College will live on. New men will fill the studies and corridors, will kneel in the lovely little Chapel, facing the blaze of glory through the Ascension window. They will feel they are compassed about with a great cloud of witnesses. From the walls the names will look down—names of Richmond men who fell on the field, fighting the good fight, calling to those who follow, the Richmond war-cry, 'Rejoice, fellow citizens! We conquer!'

A college is not simply a building—teachers and taught. It is a living fellowship, an undying tradition, an inescapable influence. Richmond men pass on, but Richmond continues herself through every age and change, and her sons join to pray that the glory that is Richmond shall never pass away.

E. S. WATERHOUSE

(Reprinted from *Methodist Recorder*, Sept. 9, 1943)

PROLOGUE

THIS is Richmond—green, wide-spreading lawns which carry the eye to the stately all-embracing arms of the stone buildings, up-standing, many-windowed, and to the lofty tower over all; lawns close-trimmed, with high trees giving gracious shade. Beautiful trees, each woven into memories that men carry to distant lands. A copper beech outside Chequers. A great mulberry tree, marking the Tutors' lawn. Yonder the white spire of St. Matthias's, where Thomas Hardy sang as a boy,—a spire reflecting every mood of the changing clouds, that you will see when you walk the river bank to pleasant Kew, or in the mighty Park beyond the College.

These lawns see much of Richmond's life. On Garden Party day gay stalls bedeck them—green-blazered men escort mothers and sisters, sweethearts, or friends from 'week-end' homes; robed Tutors add to the colour of the scene. In the warm, quiet, sunlit days which precede the struggles of the London University, those who remain for examinations study—or are deceived into thinking that they study!—on these same lawns, beguiled by the rosebuds and the singing birds. These lawns feel the impress of that swift passage to the Queen's Road gate, when some son of Richmond is 'rolled off', and his fellows, having followed him in procession to the far door, turn quickly and run to bid him farewell there. He takes their memory to India or China— these lawns and towers of Richmond, which welcomed him somewhat austerely three or four years ago, but now are his, and he part of them.

The football field is there, where men from London's colleges contest fiercely; the tennis courts are beyond, where visiting teams try their strength against that of Richmond, reinforced at times by the expert deftness of a Tutor as redoubtable here as in the abstract points of New Testament criticism! There is the Avenue, edged with trees which in their proper season give the appearance of stained glass to the door at the end of the long corridor—chestnut, laburnum, and red may. We passed along this Avenue in my time to early Sacrament on Saturdays, before the Lord's Day: thither we returned from our preaching to greet our friends again and to resume our books. Here on Quiet Days we walked back from the old Chapel, not caring to speak to even those closest friends with whom we walked, but our meditation enriched with the sense of theirs.

In olden days, you would have seen within the doors a great wide staircase. Now it is different, but Wesley still stands there calling his sons to their work. At the bottom of the stairs, at certain times, you will see long black cases, stencilled 'Hong Kong', 'Bombay', and they will remind you that Richmond does not keep her children at her side. Lecture-rooms—but how can these empty places, with maps, blackboards filled with Greek or Hebrew signs, and the rest, speak much of the spiritual joy and quiet, considering zest, the intellectual thrill that springs from the mastery of new truth? Here is the Chapel—but it needs to be filled with the deep consecrating silences of the services which mark too swiftly passing terms. To older memories it will recall the careless, resting presence of the friends who knew it as a common room, and the College meetings.

Tread these corridors with quick imagination. Behind those doors young men have dreamed and prayed and laboured—known the burning of spiritual ardours and in discussion caught another's fire. Men you have known and loved and honoured, felt their aspiration deepening within these walls, piled their books upon those shelves, decked the rooms with cushions and curtains which spoke the loving care and thought of distant homes and mothers.

> *'Lo, this room is not mine—a hundred men*
> *Sat where I sit awhile, prayed where I pray;*
> *Strong was the Mother to refresh them then,*
> *Strong is she still, to guide my feet to-day.'*

We climb to the high tower and find London open to our view, from distant Alexandra Palace to where her southern sister once caught the summer sun. Beneath us winds the river, with the tree-clad island, something that every Richmond man remembers. This is Richmond. Her sons dwell far and wide, but they remember her, love and honour her, treasure her silent behests, her leadings towards the service of her Master and theirs.

I. THE SPIRIT OF RICHMOND

RICHMOND AND 'THE FIELD'

REGINALD GLANVILLE, 1922-5

LIFE at Richmond has, for a long time now, been pervaded by the memory that this was once, in a quite especial sense, a 'missionary' college. Scarcely a student within its walls, at any time during the past fifty years, can have been oblivious of this fact or altogether unresponsive to it. Though for a longish period now no larger proportion of men has gone overseas from Richmond than from our other colleges, it is still true that in the minds of those who receive their theological training there the memory is never altogether submerged, that they are members of a fellowship which was once dedicated in its entirety to the evangelization of lands across the seas. The sources of this pervasive, communal awareness are not so simple or obvious as might be supposed. The actual period over which the Missionary Committee controlled the Institution was only a brief one, comprising no more than seventeen out of a history of a hundred years; and, furthermore, it is probable that by far the greater part of Richmond men never hear even that piece of College history overtly discussed during their term of residence there.[1] Yet it would probably be found, if examination could be made of the contents of the subconscious mind of the men in residence there at any time during the past fifty years, that the fact that missionary students were segregated there for a number of years at some time in the past was both generally and clearly apprehended. If we ask, as well we might, what could account for so general an apprehension of a fact so rarely discussed, we should be led to a number of discoveries, all interesting in themselves and cumulatively of considerable force and significance.

[1] This fact is part of the 'Traditions' which all incoming men now hear.—ED.

Not least important would be the large polished oak tablets which look down from the walls upon all who pass and re-pass in the Entrance Hall, bearing the names and country and years of service of those ex-students of Richmond who have given up their lives upon the mission field. These 'Rolls of Honour', with names dating from the earliest years of College life, point not only back, in time, to the residence within its walls of those whom they commemorate; they point outwards, also, in geogaphical space, to the lands to which they went in the constraint of the Gospel, and in which they died. Who could assess or measure the impact, through constant iteration, of their mute witness and appeal upon the tone of life of this youthful and impressionable society? There is another thing which appears to be peculiar to Richmond, which must have operated with considerable intensity in relation to the claims of the wider missionary field; this is the unity of two ceremonies, separated by the space of a few days, in which all the students share when one of their number leaves for a station overseas. There is, first, the 'Rolling Off', which takes place on the occasion of departure; then the 'Warble', a few nights later, when the missionary-to-be has actually entered upon his voyage and is known to be somewhere at sea and travelling hourly farther away from home and friends. The origins of this dual ceremony appear to be lost in obscurity, but are almost certainly as old as the College itself. Probably no year has passed since its foundation but one or more of its members has been 'rolled-off' and 'warbled', and there can be no one who ever took part in one such ceremony on whom its immediate poignancy was lost, or who was able ever altogether to forget it. If we look at this extended ceremony in its two parts, the note of the 'Rolling Off' will be recognized as one of enthusiasm; the note of the 'Warble', on the other hand, is one of solemnity. On the earlier occasion, the departing man, arm-in-arm with two of his closest friends, shakes hands with every other student as the whole body lines the main stairway. (In pre-reconstruction days the whole body of students lined the main stairway; now the ceremony is held in the main hall.) He is then conducted in procession to the north door of the main corridor, where his taxi waits to take him either to his train or to his ship lying in the dock; then, in order to greet him with the College Cry[1] as he drives away, the whole student body rushes back through the corridor and out through the main entrance and across the lawns; and the whole is shot through with the triumphant sense that Richmond has given another son to 'the Field', justifying afresh her existence to both God and man.

After the lapse of a night or two, once more, this time at night, the men assemble where they did before, each with a lighted candle in his hand; the whole chorus of male voices, unaccompanied by any instrument, joins in the valedictory hymns, 'Eternal Father' and 'Speed Thy servants, Saviour, speed them'; the entire community is penetrated and integrated by a thrilling sense of urgency, vocation and spiritual love; there is an involuntary concentration of thought and feeling upon the missionary-to-be and a drawing near in the Love of God to the land to which his journey has already begun; and there is an awareness, flooding over the threshold of the conscious mind, that in this ceremony the present is wedded to the past and the future and that all that is meant by 'Richmond' comes into its own. How much this active tradition, maintained over so long a period of time and shared in, in all probability, on more than one occasion by every one of its students, has done to sustain that noble preoccupation with 'the Field' which has marked itself so deeply upon the life of Richmond College, many tokens could be brought to demonstrate. Not least, perhaps, the brief selection of lines from the *Old Chariot* which follows will testify to the depth of the impression made by the second part of this dual ceremony—the 'Warble'—upon those who have been privileged to share in it:

> *'The stairway, lined with men, with faces grave,*
> *Singing, with import solemn, holy words . . .*
> *The candles' flickering light the sole illume*
> *Of all the faces there. . . .*
> *"Speed, speed Thy servants, Lord." . . .*

[1] See p. 154.

> *Surely we feel e'en now that those we love*
> *Rising upon the bosom of the sea*
> *Say to each other, "Now they think of us!"*
>
> *'And so shall others go;*
> *Those whom we sing have sung this hymn before,*
> *And with pure prayers sped others on the way,*
> *And we who sing to-night—where shall we be*
> *A few years hence? Perchance 'tis ours to stand*
> *Gazing into the gently heaving sea*
> *Beneath a starlit sky—to hear the soft*
> *Lapping, against the dark sides of our boat . . .*
> *Filled with a purpose high, for it is Thine;*
> *Filled with a holy love, which Thou hast given,*
> *To spend and to be spent, for others' sake. . . .'* [1]
>
> . . . . .
>
> *'The pale flames vanish; all is still;*
> *The silence grips as some strange power;*
> *The darkness fain our souls would fill,*
> *But God is here, 'tis trysting hour. . . .*
>
> *'And Souls are stirred, nor shall we fear,*
> *For His pure spirit draws us near.*
> *But now the lights flash on again,*
> *The mystic spell is broken through. . . .*
>
> *' . . . as we turn to go away*
> *There comes a voice we understand,*
> *Lo! I am with you every day,*
> *And none shall pluck you from My hand;*
> *Your friend is Mine, and I am yours;*
> *Your prayers unlock effectual doors.'* [2]

If, from things both present and past, we turn our scrutiny to things past, but present no more, we shall not be forgetful of the importance in the life of all growing, organic things of the earliest, the formative years of their existence. The

---

[1] F. H. Cumbers, *Old Chariot*, No. 23.
[2] G. N. Stephens, *Old Chariot*, No. 27.

psychology of communities is less advanced, as a subject of study, than that of individuals, but few would be prepared to deny that with them, as well, the earliest years stamp themselves decisively upon the growing organism. Though so long past, Israel has not outgrown the Exodus, nor the Church of Christ the Cross and the Open Grave. So far as Richmond is concerned, in the links that have united her in so special a sense with the missionary work of our Church, there are one or two such facts which appear to be of particular importance. For though no man or committee appears to have designed it, it is true that associations of the closest sort were forged between this 'Institution' and the Mission House from the day of its foundation, and maintained in considerable strength during all the years of its earliest growth and development. Jabez Bunting, whose position in the Connexion was one of unrivalled authority and power through the years when Richmond was in its infancy, was at that time exercising his third term of office as Secretary of the Mission House. In addition to this, he had enjoyed, since the foundation of the Theological Institution, the office of '*President of the Institution*', a privilege which gave him an unfettered right of entry into the Colleges and a considerable power of control over all those who lived and worked within them. It was true, even in those days, that the administrative offices of the Missionary Society were in fairly tolerable proximity to the Theological Institution at Richmond, and it would have been impossible, surely, for Dr. Bunting, in moving to and fro between his office and this youthful and ardent student community to keep them at the extremities of his mind? Impossible, also, for the young students in residence at Richmond, when he came amongst them, apostolic in authority and zeal, to forget who he was and whence he came. How often, one wonders, when confronted in his office by urgent claims or sudden opportunities, did he post off to Richmond to lay the work, with pleadings and prayer, before youths only too eager to respond to his appeal.[1] This is the sort of thing, at any rate, that we

[1] Many of the Tutors, too, even in modern days, have served on the field.—ED.

stumble upon in reading the Minutes of the Board of the Institution: 'Nov. 6, 1845. Mr. Hoole stated to the Board that Messrs. Henry Waite [i.e. J. H. Wayte 1845–6] and David Griffiths, two of the missionary students, had, on an unexpected emergency requiring the appointment of a Missionary to Sierra Leone and on the notice of three or four days only, voluntarily offered themselves as Missionaries to that Station; and had been removed from the Institution for the purpose of entering upon their labours as Christian missionaries in that Colony.' Or, again, from a Report under the name of the Rev. John Farrar, dated July 28, 1846: 'Two ... when the Missionary Committee were in immediate want of help, offered to go at a few days' notice to Sierra Leone. One of them shortly after his arrival was seized with the fever, and having for a while patiently endured great affliction, was removed from his earthly labour to his heavenly rest. His end was peace and joy. In his last moments he thanked God that he had been permitted to offer himself as a Missionary to Western Africa.' In such a way, through this undesigned connection, did the sense of the imperious claims of the Kingdom Overseas enter into the mind, the heart, and the will of this infant College; and what can we do but give thanks to God that its students have not outgrown it yet? The character of the mature community owes more than it probably realizes to the impressions, enthusiasms, and responses of the years of its infancy.

However that may be, the conviction appears to have developed in the minds of those responsible for our Missionary strategy that it would be a good thing to have an Institution devoted exclusively to the preparation of young candidates for service on the Foreign Field. The desirability, from their point of view, would appear to call for little demonstration. With such an Institution under their control, they would know precisely, at any time, what their resources in man-power were, and might hope to keep them proportioned to the claims of the work overseas; they would be free to go, in recurring emergencies, not in order to plead, but in order to direct. Certain it is, whatever the precise cast in which their reflections were formed, that when in celebration of the Jubilee of the Missionary Society, in the year 1863, the Methodist people raised the sum of £180,000, the Missionary Committee lost no time in making their plans for a separate Institution under their own control. An early suggestion for the erection of a new College for this purpose was abandoned for another, under which the Missionary Society purchased Richmond from the Trustees of the Theological Institution for the sum of £37,500, and endowed it with a further £20,000. It was in the year 1868 that Dr. George Osborn, relinquishing the Secretaryship of the Missionary Society, was appointed Theological Tutor at Richmond, and the control of the College by the Missionary Committee became complete. So far as can be ascertained, this change was never wholly approved by the students in the College, but it was not in the currency of the democracy of those days that these should be consulted. Hugh Price Hughes, within a year of the change, then in his fourth year as a student and speaking as Chairman of the Students' Missionary Meeting, gave public expression to their doubts and fears in a speech for which he was rewarded by the threat of the loss of two years of his probation. But time was to prove his judgement sound, for the new policy appears not to have yielded the results that were hoped, and it was not long before it became plain that any gain that accrued to the work of the Missionary Society was outweighed by loss. Returning missionaries had no ministerial friends at home, and men in other colleges had no contacts to fire their zeal in urging the missionary cause. No more than seventeen years had elapsed before there was another change; and since 1885 the College has received students indifferently as to their vocation for service at home or overseas.[1]

There is then, at Richmond, a depth and continuity of missionary devotion unexplained by the actual control of the College by the Missionary Committee for a scant seventeen years; there is an association between the Society and the College operating effectively, on the other hand, from its earliest foundation, and fruitful still. This association, of

[1] The Missionary Society held the property until 1931, when it was handed over to the Ministerial Training Committee.

which it cannot be said that it was designed by any person or by any group of persons, has issued in results so beneficent that if we would trace it back to its true source we should surely have to say that it originated in the mystery of the wisdom and the counsel of the Most High. As, in the beginning of the Gospel, Jesus 'appointed twelve, that they might be with Him, and that He might send them forth to preach', so, through a hundred years He has led young Methodists abroad from the walls of this College; and it is to His glory only, though for the salvation of the whole world, that so many of them have carried their lighted candles to the darkest corners of the earth. A text, now written up in the window of the Chapel, has always echoed within the walls of this lovely building, and has wrought with effective constraint upon many a heart: 'Go ye therefore and make disciples of all the nations.' So Richmond has proved to be one of the mansions of the Son of God, one of the 'abiding-places' of His disciples.

RICHMOND AND EVANGELISM

W. E. SANGSTER, 1920–3

FOR more than fifty years past in Methodism there have been bold and, perhaps, misguided people who have claimed so intimate a knowledge of our Church and her institutions that they have not only insisted that each of our colleges has characteristic differences from all the others, but that they could tell, with a high degree of accuracy, the college from which any minister came. So far as I know, these bold claimants have never been put to a serious test, but I have been amused to hear them assert without qualification: 'Now Didsbury is the college which produces preachers'—and I have remembered that W. Morley Punshon and W. L. Watkinson and Hugh Price Hughes and Parkes Cadman and Leslie D. Weatherhead (to mention only the first few names which come to mind) were all Richmond men. I have

heard them say: 'Now Headingley produces our scholars'—
and I have remembered that W. H. Dallinger (the only
Methodist minister to be made F.R.S.) and G. G. Findlay
and W. F. Lofthouse and Vincent Taylor were also Richmond men. 'As for Handsworth," these bright commentators affirm, "there is always something of the "gentleman"
about a man who comes from Handsworth...!!' Something!!
I was a Handsworth man myself for six months and enough
of that loyalty survives to resent the intended compliment
(def.: 'gentleman' is a man who does nothing for his living:
the word is 'hobo' in American)—and then to add the
honest 'something'!!

In my hearing, these minor psychiatrists never reached
their analysis of Richmond. Perhaps I broke up the party.
It's a pity! It would have been nice to know which way they
went wrong, but it sets me wondering what one term (if any)
I should have been glad to hear used of the men who came
from that dear place by the Thames. No happily married
man resents the wedded bliss of others. He is even secretly
glad when he hears another man assert that his wife is 'the
best in the world'. But he has no disposition to change
himself! And no Richmond man, so far as I know, ever
resented the delight with which other men speak of their
college—but he has no disposition to change! Comparisons
are odious, so he refrains from making them, but how can
he help but be adoringly grateful that it was here that he was
hammered on God's anvil and sent out to be a minister of the
Word.

And now I have the word I wanted! 'Evangelist' is the
word which would please me most if it could be honestly
used as distinctive of Richmond men. Scholarship? Yes!
But not for itself; not to be defended like 'pure maths' and
exulting in the fact that it isn't any use to anybody; not productive of the recluse who regards the normal work of the
minstry as an interruption of his researches and finishes up
knowing more about the eighteenth century than the
twentieth!

Preaching? Yes! But not preaching as a fine art; not

stylistic, essay-like compositions, pleasing to 'men of taste', polished and half-unconsciously aiming to provoke admiration for the author. But elemental preaching, with a sense of 'given-ness' all over it, drenched in prayer, clearly out to do something, challenging, all but dragging men into the presence of God and shaking 'the trembling gates of hell'.

'Evangelist' is the best word. Every true son of Richmond, wheresoever the spirit of God has sent him: among the refugees of China, teaching school in India, cutting a path through the pathless forest in Africa, fostering the work of God in the West Indies, maintaining a mission in the slums of a great city, making himself the friend of all in a group of villages, holding a central pulpit and guiding an eager pen . . . wheresoever that son of Richmond labours this word should sound, clear in his ear: 'Do the work of an evangelist.' To this test he will bring all his efforts. At the close of the day, if God spares him a little time to sit beside the fire with his life work really over, he will hold this question honestly before his eyes: 'Have I done the work of an evangelist?' If others praise him to his face, he will watch the peril of flattery and all their eulogies will melt in the crucible of his honest mind and re-shape themselves again into this question: 'Have I done the work of an evangelist?'

He will not interpret 'evangelism' narrowly. He will not think of it as belonging only to preaching, and to one kind of preaching, but he will have one sovereign test for all his endeavours: 'Has my work, and my way of life, so far as I could make them, brought people to God?'

Now, whether or not any particular man has failed or succeeded in that high enterprise must be left to the commerce of his own soul with God. But this can be said without cavil. Richmond shaped him to that end. The pious fathers who, at the first Methodist Conference in 1744, raised the question of a seminary for the training of the preachers, but had to leave it to their successors ninety years later to carry the project out, had but one thought in mind all the time: How can the preachers be made more effective evangelists? When the work was begun in Hoxton and enlarged to include

Abney House as a 'Preparatory Branch of the Institution', and when, later, a building was planned to combine both (which it was thought 'expedient to fix in the neighbourhood of London') this over-arching consideration was ever before them. Serious and scholarly as the original curriculum undoubtedly was, no one can pore over it and remain in doubt that it was all fashioned to enable men the better to do 'the work of an evangelist'.

The swiftest survey of a century's recordings makes it plain that this end was ever kept in view. It would be frank to admit that, in some periods, it appears to have been seen more clearly than at others, but at no period could a man have been honestly ignorant why this tower rose on Richmond Hill or for what purpose these young men had gathered by old Father Thames. Certainly, the neighbourhood was not in ignorance. Nearly eighty years later (in 1920) when, as a member of that happy band of brothers who had the joy of re-opening Richmond after the First World War, I went down to the riverside to make advantageous terms for the College boating, the old owner of the boats waved all my explanations as to who we were aside.

'I know 'oo yer are, sir,' he said. 'I've known yer all me life. We calls yer "The Ranters" 'ere. Yer wants to get people saived, don't yer?'

I think I blushed a bit at the time, but the *memory* of it almost ensnares me into pride.

The anxiety to get people saved runs like a golden thread through all the record of a hundred years. In the first years of the College's life the numerous references to the opening of 'new preaching rooms' and new chapels in the riverside area become almost monotonous. All the villages in the neighbourhood (Richmond was still rural then) were visited from house to house: conversation on the step and prayer in the home was the common strategy, and a tract was left as a souvenir of the call.

When the railway came to Richmond and great gangs of men employed in its construction were living in the roughest temporary shacks, the students seized the splendid chance it offered and the Gospel went forward with the line.

The College was never parochial nor even national in its outlook. A great concern for the world was in it from the start. Reginald Glanville has recounted the great story of Griffiths and Wayte,[1] and has set forth Wayte's confession of faith.

Where he led many followed. The Church in West Africa was built on the bodies of our dead missionaries, most of them from Richmond.

Nor was it only to Africa that the Spirit led them. To every field still served by the Methodist Missionary Society these gallant heralds went, and to others also, no longer reckoned as Overseas Mission Stations, or else passed over to the care of some daughter Conference. To Australia and New Zealand they travelled and to the islands of the South Seas as well.

The work at home kept pace with the work abroad. Charles Dickens's absurd caricature of a missionary enthusiast in Mrs. Jellyby, who neglected her home while she yearned over the poor natives of Borrioboolla Gha, would have found no counterpart at Richmond. In the mid-seventies, the home mission work in the neighbourhood was so zealously undertaken that it threatened to interfere with studies and had to be curtailed. By the end of the century, all the needy areas of Richmond were divided into districts for pastoral visitation and tract distribution, each district having its group of students under a 'bishop'. When the College was closed by the First World War the men were taking an eager share in the Annual Missionary Campaigns undertaken by the united theological colleges of London.

Nor did the spirit of evangelism perish, so far as Richmond was concerned, in that tragic interregnum. The post-war generation (many of whom had wallowed in the mud of Flanders and returned more sure than ever of the need of the gospel) took their share in co-operative evangelistic campaigns, as to the manner born. The Portsmouth S.C.M. Campaign of 1923 will live in the memory of many. In Richmond itself they continued to bear their own clear witness. Open-air meetings on Saturday evenings at the

[1] See p. 22.

Orange Tree became a feature of the town's life. On Sunday evenings the 'pitch' was moved to the Terrace and the choir of the College Chapel called in. The end of this decade found the men penetrating the cinemas and holding services there.

Nineteen hundred and thirty marks the beginning of a fine series of Annual Evangelistic Campaigns broken only by the closure of the College consequent on the Second World War. It is a pleasure to set down the name of the towns stirred by these fine corporative efforts: Slough, Chelmsford, Bristol, High Wycombe, Bedford, St. Albans, Guildford, Greenwich, Bexleyheath, Bletchley, and Plymouth. The campaigns followed a pattern—but were not trammelled by it. Poster parades, open-air meetings, services in most of the town churches, mass demonstrations, and house-to-house visitation.

But not all the service of Richmond caught the public eye. One of the loveliest bits of pastoral work undertaken by the men began almost casually in 1932.

Part of the immense Prince of Wales Fund raised during 1914-18 was used in building a large and dignified home on the site of the old Star and Garter Hotel for soldiers permanently disabled during the war. It borrowed the old name and became the Star and Garter Home. For twenty years the men, whose service to their country was rendered at the price of permanent invalidism and (with some) permanent pain have made a home here one minute from the College gates. In 1932 a student unobtrusively slippped in to bring cheer where it was sorely needed, and year by year the weekly visitations continued until only the closure of the College for the second time brought the work to an end.

Another tragic stream of permanently disabled men is flowing to the Star and Garter Home. In due course, by the blessing of God, another stream of Richmond students will filter in to be their friends.

RICHMOND AND THE FUTURE

Kenneth Underwood, 1938–42

The season was late summer, the beginning of the College year 1938–9. Europe was still outwardly at peace. The time had not yet come when one did not look upon the beauties of Nature without inevitably thinking of the ugliness of man. The lawns and trees and flowers of Richmond were at the height of their splendour; the College buildings, not then deprived through raids of their pinnacles, were clothed in green. The old students were returning, and everywhere one could hear shouts of welcome, laughter and excited conversations. Newcomers were arriving, and I was among those who found themselves at Richmond for the first time. It was a presage of the years to come that there was the same welcome for us as for the others. We 'freshers' soon found one another out, and on that first evening we wandered round the grounds and beside the river getting to know each other. It was the custom at Richmond to form ourselves into groups of three to five men, and we did this at once quite easily and naturally. These 'tea-clubs' were formed accidentally, for we did not know each other sufficiently to choose our companions, but they began what were for many of us the most intimate and permanent friendships we had ever known. And so, at the beginning, Richmond for me was the 'tea-club'; but it was not long before these small communities found themselves at home in the wider fellowship of the whole College. I do not think we can over-estimate the importance of this system, for it was this that gave stability and character to the whole of our College life. I was fortunate enough to stay at Richmond for a fourth year with five others when the College was officially closed, and, looking back, I see that I ended at Richmond as I had begun. My last year was, as it were, a reminder of the importance of the smaller community within the larger.

Here I would testify to the great advantage Richmond has enjoyed in receiving men of other nationalities. In recent years, West Africa, Sweden, Germany, and France have all been represented, and we were only sorry in our time that there were not more of these men, for they were great Christians and great friends, and they had much to teach us. I hope that this will be a part of post-war Richmond, and perhaps in time it may be possible for a greater number from other parts of the world to enter our Colleges, and for more of our own men to extend their training abroad.

Ideals are always touched with reminiscence and framed by experience. Hence, in looking forward to the Richmond of the future, inevitably we look back to all that was good and noble in the Richmond we knew.

Looking to the future, we who were in Richmond till she was closed, together with the great body of Richmond men who went before, pray that these things may be preserved to express in the life of future generations the fellowship and faith of our high calling. To this end, an accurate and detailed account of the 'Traditions of Richmond' has been compiled and will be passed on.[1] To a fresh body of men some of these traditions may seem meaningless, and probably this is unavoidable, for their meaning is only learnt with the years. But they have been of sufficient value in the past to make every Richmond man very anxious that they should continue. For Richmond, the future must be one with the past. The traditions built up through the years are there for the making of a new generation, and it is our confident belief that the Richmond we knew, and an even greater Richmond, will rise again, as she did after the last war.

'Tradition' is a vague word, but when we speak of it in connection with Richmond it refers to an extraordinarily vivid experience. I, for one, shall never forget the evening when our year was formally welcomed into the full fellowship of the College. As we sat in the Entrance Hall at the foot of the stairs, the story was told of home and overseas men who had gone out from this place, men who had once sat where we were sitting, whose voices had rung through these very walls, and whose fine example of service had become a part of our heritage. When Richmond is re-opened, those who

[1] Pp. 148, 157.

form her first new fellowship will find no company of men already there in residence, waiting to welcome them and to pass on to them the great traditions they themselves have learnt. A responsibility will be laid upon the new pioneers. The world will be a different place in many ways; no one at the moment can say what the peace will bring: but the pioneers of the new Richmond will know, and, should they chance to read these words, we, who will be serving at home and on the mission field, would remind them of our prayers for them, for we trust them to take up the spirit of Richmond in all that has been worthy in the past.

I suppose that every Richmond man has a different picture of the 'ideal' Richmond in his mind. I will suggest some of the points in my picture, knowing that there are others who share my views.

Here I enter upon what may prove to be controversial points, but I include them for what they are worth as coming from one who has not had the advantage (or disadvantage!) of experience. In general, they are extensions of the principle of apprenticeship which is already recognized as a part of our College life and training. I envisage, then, the possibility of including in the course of training definite periods during which groups of men would be sent to work under chosen ministers in representative places, to learn at first hand the nature and problems of pastoral work, organization, and polity in a circuit or mission. Future generations will see as one of the outstanding characteristics of our times the interest shown in children and young people. The Church must lead the way in this; therefore these periods of practical experience would lay special emphasis on child study, youth work, Sunday-school methods, the relation between the Sunday school and the Church, and the provision of the right kind of atmosphere and activity for the adolescent period. The problem of retaining the adolescent as an essential element in the life of the adult Church would also have to be studied. I do not suggest the stage at which this apprenticeship could be included, except to say that the men concerned would come back to College to discuss their experiences and pursue the theory of their practical work under the guidance of their

Tutors. I believe experiments are already being made along lines similar to these. Also it would seem to be useful for a man to have the opportunity to study the rudiments of the political, social, and economic organization and problems of his time, with special reference to the particular area in which he is going to start his ministry, whether that be at home or abroad.

Finally, at Richmond, contacts should be encouraged with the theological and other colleges of London University. The geographical position of Richmond may tempt her to think of herself as self-contained and exclusive, and to forget the tremendous benefits that accrue from fellowship with others. Contact with the neighbouring theological colleges will not only lead to the establishment of friendships, but will arouse discussion on and study of the ecclesiastical and doctrinal bases of other denominations, and this is surely essential to a true unity and understanding between the various Christian bodies. And contact with colleges which represent other faculties than theology will bring Richmond men into touch with different branches of knowledge and the contemporary movements of thought.

I realize that what is new in these suggestions is mainly an extension and adaptation of the present curriculum; but nevertheless I think this would be valuable. The difficulty arises in finding time for them, but once the need for them is recognized this difficulty could be overcome.

Having had my say, I should acknowledge that there are many different points that others would have raised had they been writing this. I do not therefore claim that my picture is a comprehensive one, but rather that it is intended to be suggestive.

The year 1943 is one of great memories for Richmond. But it is typical of her genius that those who have been entrusted with the task of celebrating and recording her centenary desire, not only to look back, but to look forward, and have therefore asked that this chapter should be written. We do not know how wide the gap of intervening years will be before the College is re-opened, but we who were with her when she closed want to do all we can to bridge that gap for the sake of those who will be starting afresh in the place we have learned to love so much. It would be a tragedy for a new Richmond to grow up entirely cut off from the old. It would not bring her freedom, for she would be deprived of the greatest source of inspiration available for her. The Richmond of the future must take the torch from the hands of the Richmond of the past; she must bear it in her own way, but she must keep it burning, and pass it burning on to her successors. And what is this torch? It is the distinctive fellowship and tradition of which I have written, and it is symbolized for us in the words of the College war-cry: Ω ΣΥΜΠΟΛΙΤΑΙ ΧΑΙΡΕΤΕ ΝΙΚωΜΕΝ—'O fellow citizens, rejoice. We conquer!' This is the symbol which above all others binds Richmond together. Wherever Richmond men meet, in England or at the ends of the earth, it is understood and recognized as the symbol of their fellowship in Christ and of their common heritage. Our custom was to use it to bid 'God speed!' to the men who were leaving College to go out into the work of the Church, and it has spread throughout the world. And so we of the past address ourselves to the men of the future, and we give to you this promise, that when the College resumes her task we shall be with you in our thoughts and prayers; as you walk her corridors a cloud of witnesses will be about you, and there will be ringing in your ears the words with which we are bidding you, in your turn, 'God speed!'—ω ΣΥΜΠΟΛΙΤΑΙ ΧΑΙΡΕΤΕ ΝΙΚωΜΕΝ.

II. THE PLACE

THE STORY OF RICHMOND

FRANK CUMBERS, 1927–31

I

IT is bright and fair at Richmond on the morning of this long-anticipated day—Friday, September 15, 1843. Three hundred of us have just arisen from an excellently furnished breakfast table, with the proper sense of well-being which arises from a good breakfast and a sense of good works ahead. Now we wait for one o'clock and the opening ceremonies, and meantime we have leisure both to survey our new Theological Institution, and to meditate upon the things which have led us to this day, and upon the arguments as to the wisdom of it all which still rise high wherever Methodists meet.

Some of us have long favoured the scheme. We have often reminded the hesitant how Mr. Wesley introduced the matter at his very first Conference. As Mr. Gaulter said at Conference some years ago: 'It is novel to call this a novel project. I have heard it talked about ever since I came to Conference.' Despite this, we have waited for ninety years; only eight years ago was the seminary opened. It is sad to think to-day that Dr. Adam Clarke has not lived to see this glorious answer to the pleas he made so strongly, nearly forty years ago—not to mention the Northern Branch at Didsbury, now working so well.

It has been an anxious question through many Conferences, and may continue so. We who rejoice to-day have long been urging that Methodism's vastly growing parish, and the improved standards of her people, point to a need for trained preachers. Why should proper training quench the flame of evangelical zeal? Yet others, we confess, speak weightily when they point to the bright triumphs of an 'untrained ministry'. After all, we have increased from 71,463 to 451,286 between 1790 and 1843.

We remember the anxious debates before Hoxton was opened. Some expressed fears as to the effects of this thing upon the characters of our young preachers. Was it right to enforce celibacy upon them? And college life is notoriously dangerous to young men, said others. And do we need all our ministers in one mould? Will not erudition take the place of sound conversion? And will not the college-trained take a pompous air upon them? May not a desire for accuracy overbear the longing for heavenly unction?[1]

But many of these fears were allayed when Mr. Joseph Entwisle and Mr. John Hannah were given charge, and when Dr. Bunting was appointed 'President'. We have heard Mr. Entwisle himself confess that at first he thought the young preachers would learn more, and learn better, out in the work, under the guidance of judicious superintendents. But he has come to 'feel most firmly that the arrangement is providential'. We have read the words of shrewd advice which he offers to his young men,[2] and realize that any minister and Methodist among us would be advantaged by them. Mr. Joseph Hunt has spoken with conviction too. 'I entered upon my great work', he says, 'in a very raw, unfinished state, and little do the opposers of the Divinely-approved Institution know of the difficulties with which such as I have had to contend, through the whole of our ministerial labours, to this day. We have had, as it were, to live from hand to mouth, and gather our knowledge as we could. . . . Hence how many months have been comparatively lost when reading books not to our purpose.'[3]

We feel to-day that Hoxton has served us well, and that the two years of our 'preparatory school' at Abney House have also been a very great advantage. To be sure, Hoxton has been stigmatized as 'mean and dark': an irreverent spirit even declared that the premises 'bore no very distant resemblance to a series of gloomy pigeon-holes'!

---

[1] See letter from James Wood to Joseph Entwisle, p. 400, Entwisle's *Memoirs*.
[2] Pp. 403 ff., *ibid*.   [3] P. 420, *ibid*.

Mr. Entwisle has been meeting the young men in class at Hoxton, and has done much for them. And since he left the seminary five years ago, Mr. Treffry has carried on his work in the same good way. They have both done much to allay the fears of Methodists about the Institution's work. And London chapels have heard the young men preach and know their worth; the passers-by in the streets have heard them in the open air.

So well, indeed, has the Institution succeeded that it has earned the right to better resources and surroundings. Some students have been boarded out with the preachers, some at long distances, which does not make for convenience. Despite all difficulties, Methodism has begun to feel that all its preachers must be college-trained; yet how we should have aspired to this it would be hard to say but for the great Centenary Fund—for of the £221,939 which it raised, Conference devoted £75,300 to the Theological Institution Fund.

As we tread these bright lawns to-day, we feel some pride in belonging to a Church which, having raised nearly a quarter of a million for its Centenary, puts a third of it to the training of its ministers and another third to the cause of missions!

Debates in high places overshadowed the issue. We remember the attacks on Dr. Bunting, who is to speak to us to-day. It is eight years now since Dr. Warren left us after his astonishing reversal of policy—from eager support of the colleges to the forming of associations and leagues against them. As we have seen, Mr. Entwisle himself was very doubtful of the working of a scheme perhaps purposely left vague; but we know what great work Dr. Bunting has done, though it has not surprised us, knowing his wonderfully happy and attractive manner with young men. We know that Dr. Bunting neither expected nor desired the suggestion that he should be both President of the Institution and Theological Tutor as well, and the selector of the staff generally.

But as we turn upon these lawns it is difficult to occupy ourselves with past history any longer, and all our mind goes to consider this beautiful and dignified place in its detail. The surroundings are charming—nor shall we fall into the heresy of fearing lest natural beauty shall turn studious minds from their true task. Squire Williams's manor house and grounds have formed a good foundation, and Mr. Trimen, our architect, has given of his best. It did seem at one time that the Institution would be built at Hampstead. We remember reading a letter from Mr. Treffry:[1] 'I believe it is pretty nearly determined . . . to have our new Institution erected on a spot of ground about a mile to the west of Hampstead Heath and two miles from the extreme part of Regent's Park. The situation is pleasant. But I objected to it on the following grounds. It is on the Finchley Road, where there is no gas, no police, scarcely any population, no chapel nearer than a mile and a half',—but the Committee carried it largely, after a discussion of some hours. Well, there would have been some advantages in Hampstead, for perhaps —who knows?—the march of future years may bring civilization even to the Finchley Road, and banish the memory of highwaymen from Finchley Common. But who to-day could question the wisdom that brought us here? As we stand and admire, a knowledgeable friend expatiates on the rarity and beauty of the trees Squire Williams planted—fir and stone pine, deciduous cypress and ailanthus, elm and sycamore and chestnut—and two acres of lawn. Some of these trees are rarely seen in England, he tells us. Did we but know it, there are trees within our view to-day which will cause grave perturbation, solemn resolutions and appeals from the students to the Committee, in years to come; but how are we to dream in this year of grace that in another fifty brief years our students will want to play football on the field yonder, and will find the trees in their way?[2]

Now the building takes our eye. A beautiful stately erection in Bath stone has been joined to the old manor house. We are impressed by its square tower, the octagonal turrets,

---

[1] *W.H.S. Proceedings*, II, Pt. 1, p. 27, 1899.

[2] A petition is preserved dated June 3, 1891, asking for the removal of the beech tree situated almost in the middle of the field. An austere tutorial pencil has altered 'beech' to 'lime'!

the battlemented walls and mullioned windows. (Who are we to guess that future generations of guardians will ruefully consider again and again heavy expense in reconditioning those battlements and that beautiful stonework? Far less could we dream that in a hundred years' time invaders of the upper air will shake them perilously.) On the ground floor there is a fine entrance hall, dining-hall and the lecture-rooms; on the first floor a central library and studies, and on the second floor are bedrooms. A future Principal is destined to declare sadly that what comprised 'every requisite' for 1843 will hardly be serving as effectively for 1932! But in our pride to-day we are not likely to imagine that this Institution and its sisters will be so starved in the matter of upkeep by the Methodist people as in fact they are to be, until Ritson and Lamplough arise for their succouring. To-day, then, we are very satisfied. The building, Mr. Trimen tells us, measures 248 feet by 65, and between the wings there is a run of 165 feet. As we stand within, at one end of the great corridor, we have a vista of 230 feet. Back in the grounds again, we wonder what will happen to the orangery and vinery. These *are* perhaps a little too luxurious for Methodist preachers.

But one o'clock approaches, and committee, ministers, students, and friends all enter the large lecture-room together. Our preacher enters—Dr. Jabez Bunting, President of the Institution, a 'prince in Israel', indeed, about whom so much of praise and of blame has been voiced. To most of us here to-day, however, he represents much that is greatest in Methodism; his accomplishments seem endless. We have come to feel that nothing is complete without him, that all he touches is admirably done. This Institution owes much to his vision, large-mindedness and governing skill. A young man named George Osborn, too, is taking due note of all he does, as though determined to take him for his exemplar.

Our meeting begins. Dr. Bunting announces the Hymn 744,[1] 'The Saviour, when to heaven He rose . . .' and we sing

[1] No. 750 in 1904 book, and yet another of the illustrious company of casualties from the present collection.

these words, thinking of the 'bright succession' and the 'unborn churches' which shall rise under the guidance of the young men in our midst to-day, and those who shall come after them. The same thought seems to be with all, and the hymn goes well. The Rev. Joseph Sutcliffe prays, and then Dr. Bunting rises for his address. He is in good spirit for it. 'Our main business', he says, 'is to praise God for these new blessings, and to offer prayer to Him for the success and prosperity of both branches of the Institution. But there are certain things which I must say first!' He speaks of the beauty of the surroundings, and then declares that to-day there will be no eloquent speeches. 'Methodist preachers have not time for their elaboration; besides, I like the simplicity of Methodism—and I hope that it will be remembered in the object of our present concern.' (Approving murmurs.) He goes on to tell us that he greatly objects to this place being called Richmond College. 'It is Richmond Institution, or, more diffusely, the Richmond Branch of the Wesleyan Theological Institution.' Wesley desired a seminary for his young preachers; now, after a century, the proper means are at hand. 'Admittedly the Institution is still in the experimental stage, having had eight years of life only; but I make bold to say that it has been a successful and encouraging experiment.' He speaks of the House Governor's task, his duty of general superintendence, a sort of wardenship of premises and men alike. He would have called such a person the 'Chaplain'. His address ends with an appeal for financial support. Obviously (he says) those who have given one pound for the support of an institution with thirty students should surely give two pounds to support two institutions with seventy-six students! (In this conclusive syllogism, the unuttered premise is, of course, 'We can always rely upon the Methodist people to give where there is need'.)

Now Dr. Dixon speaks. He declares himself, amidst our approving laughter, 'thunderstruck' to find himself, a Wesleyan minister, 'located in this beautiful edifice, surrounded by a royal park, and near a more than royal river!' He stresses the need for all learning to be vitalized by love of God. 'If we wish the young men whom we are about to train, to be scholars, we must keep them close to God; if we wish them to be acute and profound thinkers, we must keep them close to the Bible; if we wish them to be eloquent, their hearts must be filled with divine love.' Mr. Burton speaks, and so does Mr. Thomas Farmer, who lives over at Gunnersbury House, and is already showing himself a friend of the Institution. Our meeting closes with the Benediction from the President of the Conference, after Dr. Bunting has read 2 Timothy iv to us.

The officials seem to be conferring as we stream out, and soon it is announced that, after all, our afternoon service will be, not in Richmond Chapel, but out on the lawn. Certainly the crowd seems too big for the Chapel, and nothing could be more appropriate than an open-air service. The weather holds, and after the fervent and powerful prayer of Thomas Jackson, John Scott, the President, speaks to us from Psalm iv. 3: 'Know that the Lord has set apart him that is godly for Himself.' Then, with renewed prayer, we leave, feeling that we have done good work to-day.

Richmond has begun.

II

It had been intended to build Richmond first. The now faded Record Book of students is lettered 'Hoxton and Richmond', and the memorial tablet to Calvert and Hunt of Hoxton and Fiji is at Richmond. On the other hand, John Hannah went from Hoxton to Didsbury. Which sets a pretty problem: Which is the premier Wesleyan college? (But every minister can answer that.)

'The college is a fine building in Perpendicular style,[1] standing on the top of Richmond Hill, in an estate of about 11 acres. With the important reservation of a somewhat enervating climate, the place is in all respects admirably adapted to its purpose. The great sweep of the lawn in front of the college is an abiding means of grace. For some of us, memories of our textual and theological disasters recall, by way of compensation, the scent of wallflowers and daffodils

[1] Thomas Stephenson, *Methodist Magazine*, 1906, p. 537.

wafted through the windows some warm spring morning!' He adds that within the college something had been sacrificed to the imposing style of the architecture, and that improvements to the comfort of the place, and necessary enlargements, have only been made with great difficulty.

It was soon felt that a College chapel was necessary; the scheme was begun with £1,000 from the Connexion, and a public appeal which did not succeed. It was expected to cost £2,000; Mr. Thomas Farmer defrayed an additional £482 1s. 3d., and certainly some of the other expense. A word is in place here regarding this early benefactor of Richmond. As a child, he went begging from door to door for missions with Dr. Coke, and in his memoirs Thomas Jackson refers to Farmer as 'the most striking example I have ever known of sanctified prosperity'. The records of early days reveal instance upon instance of his desire to adorn the College. His next important gift was the statue of John Wesley.

This fine marble work shows Wesley in gown and bands, Bible in hand and in the attitude of preaching—though it is demurred that Wesley never raised his index finger while preaching! It is considered to be a masterly likeness, and we have 'chapter and verse' for this important matter in the testimony of Dr. Adam Clarke, set down in 1830 at the request of the President. He declared that in 1781 Wesley gave five sittings to Wood of Burslem, and that Wesley was thoroughly satisfied with the result. Dr. Clarke had Wood's model cast in brass by John Forshaw, chased up to the original under John Jackson, R.A., and he lent the model to Samuel Manning. 'The noble appearance of his face', says Clarke, 'I see in the terra-cotta of Mr. Wood, and exactly transferred from it to the clay and afterwards to the selenite of Mr. Manning.' (In *W.H.S. Proceedings*, 1908, the Rev. R. Green queries the exactness of this likeness.) The model by Samuel Manning was exhibited in the Academy in 1828, and the statue was commissioned, but never completed. In 1830 a site was requested for the statue in Westminster Abbey, but Dean Ireland refused this 'on account of the factious character of Mr. Wesley'.

It was the sculptor's grandson, also Samuel, who executed the work. The statue was installed on June 14, 1849, the occasion being celebrated by a public breakfast at the Star and Garter! Within two years it was decided that the statue was in the wrong place—'for want of proper light its merits could not be fully seen'—and Mr. Farmer gave another £200 to pay for the removal.

Thomas Jackson came into possession of the Foundery pulpit, and this was installed on November 20, 1856. We may mention here the names of Isaac Holden and James S. Budgett, whose gifts are frequently mentioned in early records. At the 1932 re-building, a 'Book of Benefactions' has been instituted, where we read of the Shrubsall Chair (Systematic Theology), the Edmund Lamplough Chair of New Testament Language and Literature and Classics, the Mr. and Mrs. Herbert Walker Chair (Philosophy). Edmund Lamplough also gave the organ in the College Chapel, and Lord Wakefield the stained-glass window by Frank Salisbury. Large donations for Prize Funds have been made by such friends as Canon Cornwall Jones, James Howard Westcott, W. T. Davison and J. T. Smart. An older prize benefaction, and for many years the only one, is the Jenkins Prize. Mention should be made, too, of the consistent support afforded to the College by Mr. John Finch.

Other points concerning the fabric of the building may be added.[1] The Manor House itself was adapted for the House Governor and the Theological Tutor. Richmond men remember with amusement the Theological Tutor who (it is said) demanded the transference of the large Georgian porch from the Governor's front door to his own! Certain dairy buildings in the grounds were made into a house for the Classical Tutor, John Farrar. It made, says Dr. Barber, a damp but very pretty cottage. 'The winding paths between [the lawns] led to our house,' Miss Anna M. Hellier has written, 'low-roofed and all but hidden among the trees. It was an enlarged cottage, the older house whitewashed, and the rest of it covered with large-leaved ivy where birds nested, and on early summer mornings woke us by their

[1] See also Dr. Barber's *Short History*.

fluttering to and fro, the sound of baby bird voices. Round the latticed porch, white roses, clematis and jessamine climbed to its roof.' Another member of the family has spoken of the 'well-kept lawns, beautiful in spring with their wealth of flowering shrubs, in summer with their brilliant flower-beds and borders, and at all times with their stately trees'. But Dr. Geden[1] once spoke candidly of a time when things were not so, and while paying tribute to the beauty seen in his day, mentioned a former time when the donkey was tethered on the lawns, and the flower-beds contained little but weeds! The present College Villa was built in 1893 (now called 'the Principal's House').

When an old student casts his mind's eye over the grounds, he will see Brixton's squarish figure striding steadily across the lawn. This 'good and faithful servant" will complete fifty years' service in July, 1944, and has been head gardener for more than half that time. He knows all about the soil—and the sub-soil—and can tell much about the men and Tutors. For instance, there is the story how he and Dr. Waterhouse and one or two more captured a stag that had wandered in from the Park! Our story would be incomplete indeed if we left out 'the Brixtons', for they too are lovers of Richmond.

Thomas Jackson's library of 7,500 volumes was purchased by James Heald in 1859 and given to the College. There is also a small collection of books which belonged to Fletcher of Madeley. There have been transactions over the estate, and alterations to the buildings; the land bordering on Friar's Stile Road was leased to the Corporation in 1892; one of the houses built on this land was later acquired for the Tutor in New Testament and Classics (1921). The Lycett Room (given by Sir Francis Lycett) was added by 1898, together with some new baths, badly needed. Modern builders will hear with envy that it cost £245, plus £35 for furnishing! This room greatly aided the work of the College (there being only three lecture-rooms for five Tutors), and the old Library (now the Chapel) looked all the better for the removal of the two bookstands which had occupied the

[1] *Old Chariot*, No. 3.

middle of the floor. In 1903 the wings of the College were raised another story without detracting from the general effect. The old Library was adapted for use as a Common Room in 1913; since the rebuilding there is a separate Common Room.

Richmond has been well served by its generations of Committee members, and their task has often been difficult. The same meeting which considered Richmond's acquisition by the Missionary Society in 1863 heard of the necessity to repair the central staircase, whose steps 'were worn and weakened by the constant traffic of twenty-two years'. The disadvantages of converting old property were often experienced, not least when an old barrel-drain under Dr. Beet's house was discovered to be almost past repair, and had to be dealt with at great expense. On several occasions the stonework which is the glory of the beautiful front has needed costly and extensive attention and repair—the turrets and battlements have proved very susceptible to weather. We read in the College magazine of a Governor who had this matter so much at heart that he would wander on the roof by night, armed with a stick, with which he was wont to knock off pieces of the stone, to the imminent peril of latecomers at the college doors (or windows!) beneath.

We read of bills for £364 in 1895, £850 in 1919, £650 in 1936. The heating of the College, too, has always been a problem—one which has in its time gained the tribute of a lengthy description in the Committee's Minutes—there were loud noises which at one time even disturbed lectures.[1]

As the years passed, many longed for Richmond to be modernized, and as Headingley was not yet re-opened there were more men, and the congestion became acute. In 1926 thirty of the bedrooms were arranged to accommodate two men each, so that each man could have a separate study—a very desirable thing. Four years later an informal conversation among interested people outlined the scheme now so triumphantly brought into being.

The Richmond rebuilding, however, was but part of a magnificent struggle, described so admirably by Dr. Howard·

[1] Mr. T. H. Barratt's views will be found in the Didsbury Centenary volume! See also *Old Chariot* for 1921, p. 92.

that we make no apology for a lengthy quotation:[1] 'During the Rev. J. H. Ritson's Presidency in 1925-6 he felt moved to call the attention of the Methodist people to the extraordinary neglect into which it had allowed the care of ministerial training to fall. For nearly half a century no special effort had been made beyond the building of Wesley House, Cambridge, by the private generosity of two laymen. Not a penny had been allowed to go to the Fund when a million guineas were raised at the beginning of the century. Dr. Ritson flung himself into the effort of raising a fund of a quarter of a million to endow most of the Chairs at the Colleges, and to carry out some long overdue structural alterations in the fabric of the four Wesleyan colleges. It was not a popular appeal to the Methodist public, but a special appeal to a limited number of Methodists who were alive to the urgent need. Mr. E. S. Lamplough became Lay Treasurer of the Fund. The story of Mr. Lamplough's heroic struggles, together with Dr. Ritson, to raise that vast sum will never be fully told. His personal liberality is only part of a noble and sacrificial devotion. At each of the four colleges of the Wesleyan Church, a Lamplough Chair was endowed, involving a gift of £10,000 for each. In addition, each of the colleges had a chapel, and how much of the cost of building these homes of prayer came out of Mr. Lamplough's own pocket only the Treasurers know. As long as Methodism endures and its splendid theological colleges continue to train men for the ministry of the Christian Church, the names of Ritson and Lamplough will be honoured as among the greatest benefactors of our Church.'

Perhaps we may express the hope that from the reading of such words, some reader may find his or her 'concern' in this mighty work, and help to see that never again shall our care for the colleges fall so low.

The chief results, then, of the rebuilding, were the Library, the Chapel, the Common Room and the Games Room. The old Library, on the first floor above the main entrance, has been transformed into a Chapel, and by the genius of Mr. Maufe, the architect, it is now a gem among

[1] *Methodist Magazine*, 1935, p. 390.

sanctuaries of this kind. It was opened on January 12, 1932, and since the importance of the occasion demanded that the President should open it, all Richmond men were happy that the President should be Dr. Ryder Smith. Taking for his text 1 Kings viii. 27, he said: 'If we use the opportunity of this Chapel aright, then as we scatter here and there in England, and far away over the seas, the thoughts of Richmond men, generation after generation, will turn to a particular spot, and as they turn, the whole earth will be full of His glory. Holiness, love, and conviction; these three mean that the glory of the Lord is revealed.' The Communion service was presented by the men of the College, Dr. Ryder Smith's name being associated with this gift. Wesley's pulpit has been transferred from the Prayer Room. Dr. Ritson has spoken of the silence and beauty of this blue-green shrine, with its ceiling patina of gold stars. The casual visitor, he says, cannot enter without feeling 'Lo, God is here; let us adore!' The impressive stained-glass window, desgined by Mr. Frank Salisbury, was presented by Lord Wakefield. The new library is a very remarkable room indeed (see picture opposite). A short new study corridor has been allotted to the College Chairman and other officials, and is called 'Whitehall'.

III

Interesting sidelights on the march of time are to be discerned in the records of the College. Imagine the scene when on September 27, 1900, the Committee considered an application from the National Telephone Company to erect a pole near the College Chapel in Friar's Stile Road! The application was declined. However, 'the earnest wish of several gentlemen living near the college' prevailed at the December meeting, although the Committee condemned the hustling methods of a Governor who had given permission for the laying of a lead pipe without its authority! Thirteen years later we read of the possibility of electric lighting—an improvement not effected until 1919, under Dr. Workman's tenancy, at a cost of £1,000. Nineteen hundred and fourteen brought a warning from the police that suffragettes might be expected to do some damage to the property, and a watchman patrolled the grounds during the vacation. But there were other alarms in 1914.

At the October 1 meeting, Dr. Davison reported that five students were already in the Forces. Enlistment was left to individual discretion, but there was drill instead of football, under the instruction of a 'Color-Serjeant' at 5s. a time! By March, 1915, twenty-two men had left the College since September—twelve for the Forces and ten called out; thirty-five remained. Again and again at 'Seats' there were re-elections to various offices 'as —— has enlisted for the War'.

In 1915 Westminster Training College applied for the premises, as the Australian Forces had commandeered Horseferry Road. Richmond men went to Didsbury in October, and the new régime installed itself and its effects with the aid of a convoy of twenty-six vans from the Army and Navy Stores, pronounced the Richmond beds 'terrible' and brought their own. W. T. Davison continued in the Theological Tutor's house, meditating upon past glories, and serving the College Chapel—filling it for the first time for years. Westminster brought ninety-five students, taxing the accommodation to the full; they had only a brief time at Richmond before the Services claimed them, and meantime put in 'pre-Service training', not least on the football field, which, made into allotments, was apportioned among the students, members of the Chapel congregation, and some others, among whom was the redoubtable figure of J. Alfred Sharp. 'One member of the Committee who knew the College grounds well, said that in Richmond they could grow almost anything excepting potatoes!' but Dr. Workman tells us that potatoes did grow. What would the Committee of those days have said, could they have seen the field to-day, uprooted for a second time, with the land-girls busy upon it!

A note of things to come appears in the decision (June, 1916) to raise the insurance for fear of air raids, though this was not so direly urgent a matter as now. We thank God that so far the College has not suffered greatly from bombs, though incendiaries, falling plentifully, have been 'promptly dealt with'. The worst onslaught was in September, 1940, when four or five times in a fortnight the district was raided, and at teatime on September 9, thirty-two high-explosive bombs fell within 400 yards of the College. One fell in the College gardens, to the west of the villa, which had a remarkable escape. It is estimated that this did £1,000 worth of damage to the College fabric, loosening pinnacles and turrets, so that they had to be taken down.

Westminster left in 1920, though towards the end of the period it was the 'remnants' of twenty teachers' training colleges that Richmond entertained. Richmond men had been trickling back for some time and Drs. Workman and W. T. Davison lectured to them. During Westminster's stay, Dr. Workman faced the tasks of making good, at the cost of the Richmond Committee, of course, the stonework, of installing electric light, new heating apparatus and the telephone—this latter to the dismay of W. T. Davison, who would say wrathfully, 'Directly you leave, we'll pull *that* thing out!' The College re-opened on October 8, 1920.

The lists of officers in the Students' Minutes also reflect the march of time. A 'College Electrician' first appears in 1929; there is a League of Nations Secretary; while the present war brought into office a 'Sugar Curator', who made arrangements by which each student received his individual allowance! Wireless was late in its appearing, tutors and students alike seeming very justly to have been concerned with the possible interruption of studies. The students blacked-out the College before term commenced in 1939.

In 1940 Richmond welcomed thirteen men from Handsworth, and in 1941 when the College was taken over for the war period by London University, six men of the third year remained, while the second year went to Headingley and the first to Hartley-Victoria. The latest College Secretary, S. C. Fittall, has left an interesting account of the last year's life. The six men maintained all the College traditions so far as possible—and seem to have acted very worthily of such a charge. Lectures, writes Fittall (somewhat cryptically), were arranged 'as necessary'. The men lived in the College House, had meals in the Dining Hall with members of the University Administrative Staff, and discussed College business in tea-club or study. Morning prayers were held in the Common Room, evening prayers, which some University

Staff attended, in the Chapel. There was a Communion Service on alternate Saturdays.

So twice has Richmond seen her sons removed since that sunny day in the 'hungry forties' when her life began. But she knows that with the passing of these days her task will be resumed. In a prosaic sense, the College Committee in 1919 defined this as a permanent necessity; 'in view of the importance of the connection already established between Richmond and Methodism in London and the south of England, and the great importance of the connection between Richmond and London University . . . it is essential that Richmond should continue its work'. In every other sense, too, every son of Richmond, and all who have received something from Richmond's sons, know that she must always be.

IV

Richmond's Jubilee was properly celebrated fifty years ago. On a day which 'could have been brighter', but with little rain until the evening, Dr. W. F. Moulton preached at a morning service, basing his words on the same text 'from which the wise, strong, faithful John Scott preached on the opening day'. In the afternoon there was a garden party, which included a cricket match (showing progress in at least one direction since the opening day), after which Dr. Rigg unveiled a bust of George Osborn, and Daniel Sanderson and he paid tribute to Osborn's work. There was an evening meeting, at which George Fletcher presented greetings from Didsbury, and displayed the ancient roll-book (doubtless under the complacent eyes of Daniel Sanderson, who had brought it up to date after a lapse of many years). John Walton, Agar Beet, J. G. Tasker also spoke, and young Isaac Shimmin, on furlough from South Africa and barely ten years out from College, paid his tribute to Richmond.

Some who read this will have shared in that scene, as some present at the Centenary will witness Richmond's one hundred and fiftieth birthday. May we so live that they may look back on us with the same affection that we bear for these honoured names.

V

It was bright and fair again at Richmond on the morning of Wednesday, September 15, 1943. The 'shadow celebration'[1] began with a service in the new Chapel, and about a hundred were there. The lawns and grounds looked well for wartime days (but we must applaud the efforts of Dr. Waterhouse and Mr. Brixton to make them so).

We started our service with Falcon Street; our other hymns were 979, 824 (vv. 1–2), the *Te Deum*, 402 (vv. 1, 3), 745 and 807. Professor Clogg read Mark vi. 6–13, 30–4, and Dr. Waterhouse led us in prayer, praise and remembrance. 'The less man touches this service, the better!' said Dr. Church, the President, and very much moved by the occasion, he spoke of Richmond's meaning. Taking Philippians iii. 20, he made his points from the versions: 'Our "conversation", "citizenship", "living" is in heaven.' 'We are a colony of heaven.' Eschewing the use of Richmond names, and drawing freely on his memory of foreign students who, having come among us, would always bear in their souls 'a little bit of Richmond', he moved us deeply to a true perception of what Richmond is and means. We moved slowly from the Chapel, friend acclaiming friend, to Hall for the tea, and for the speeches. Both were excellent.

T. H. Barratt and C. Ryder Smith spoke for former Tutors; Owen Spencer Watkins, Weatherhead, Sangster and Underwood for the generations of students. *Dr*. Dimond (surely a new dignity was never announced under more fitting conditions!) spoke for the other colleges. We perceived that our meeting, for all its joy and deep satisfaction, was symbolic of two greater things: the day when Richmond, re-opening, shall be itself again, and of that grand day when all Richmond men will meet in the final Re-union. Dr. Church had recalled F. W. Kellett's last word (see p. 123). It is a fitting prayer for us all.

[1] See *Methodist Recorder*, September 23, 1943.

THE TREASURES OF RICHMOND

I. THE RICHMOND WESLEYANA[1]

C. RYDER SMITH

1. *The Foundery Pulpit.* This is still in use here for daily worship. It bears a brass plate with the following inscription:

'In this pulpit the Revds. John and Charles Wesley preached for many years the Gospel of the Grace of God. It stood originally in the place of worship called the Foundry, situate in Moorfields, London. It came afterwards into the possession of the Rev. Thomas Jackson, and was by him presented to the Trustees of the Wesleyan Theological Institution in the year 1856. May the Students who now occupy it emulate these holy men in the zeal and fidelity with which they sought to turn many unto righteousness!'

2. *The 'Horsley' Portrait of Wesley* (see p. 54).

3. *The 'Manning' Statue.* (Dr. Smith here inserted the statement prepared some years ago by the Rev. F. B. Clogg, which has been included in the account on p. 42.) It appears that this is the earliest statue of Wesley. Mr. Frank Salisbury used Wood's bust when painting his recent picture.

4. *The Olave (or Olive) Portrait* (see p. 55).

5. *A Letter of John Wesley, dated February* 14, 1787. This will be found under that date in Telford's *Letters of John Wesley*. With this may be named an Ordination Certificate, dated in 1788, and signed by Wesley, authorizing one of his preachers, James Bogie, to administer the Sacrament.

6. *Two Class Tickets*, found in a book of Charles Wesley's with 'March 1765' written on each in his writing. There is nothing else on them but a picture of Jesus washing Peter's feet. One picture is red and the other black.

7. *The Wesley Library*, as it is here called. It was given to the college by Thomas Jackson. The books of the 'Library' are as follows:

[1] Reprinted from *W.H.S. Proceedings*, 1937, p. 57.

(a) 174 volumes which bear internal evidence that they belonged to John Wesley. Either 'John Wesley' or 'J. W.' or some other words occur in these in John Wesley's autograph. In a number he has made marginal comments, and in others press corrections. I may mention in passing that they include his copies of Bengel's *Gnomon*, and of Bengel's Greek Testament, and of a German hymn-book, which he seems to have acquired at Herrndyke in the Low Countries, on his journey to Moravia. Most of these books bear a red oval stamp, 'Methodist Chapel House Library, City Road, London'.

(b) Two hundred and ninety-two volumes which bear similar evidence that they belonged to Charles Wesley or to one of his relatives. Among the latter the most frequent names are those of his wife, his son Charles, and his daughter Sarah, but 'Samuel Wesley' (his brother), 'Rebecca Gwynne' and 'Patty Wesley' also occur. Charles Wesley's daughter Sarah, or 'Sally', lived till 1828 (*Journal*, vi, p. 328). Two or three of her books bear dates as late as 1814. Not more than one or two of the books of this 'Charles Wesley Group' have the City Road stamp named above. A number of autograph hymns are included in these volumes —for instance 'Hark! how all the welkin rings'.

8. *One hundred and twenty-one Volumes that belonged to 'Fletcher of Madeley'*. Some of these have his autograph, some his wife's, and some Miss Tooth's as well. Almost all have written inscriptions of the following kind, with small variations,—'Presented to the Wesleyan Theological Institution by Mrs. Legge, executrix of Miss Tooth, of Madeley.' One or two of these inscriptions are dated 'Dec. 4, 1843'.

9. There are besides 323 volumes which bear no 'internal evidence' of ownership or which bear early Methodist names other than the above. Many of these have the City Road stamp. A more minute examination may remove some from this class to one of those above, for I have made no attempt to examine every volume page by page.

10. *Thomas Jackson's Library*. This was purchased by Mr. James Heald, of Stockport, and given to the Theological

54   RICHMOND COLLEGE

Institution in 1859. Thomas Jackson was, I suppose, the most eager collector of Wesleyana of his time. The dates about him have some significance. He was born in 1783, entered the Methodist ministry in 1804, was Connexional Editor from 1824 to 1843, Theological Tutor at Richmond from 1843 to 1861, and died in 1873. While he was at the Book Room, he may easily have known Charles Wesley's surviving daughter, and it is likely enough that our Charles Wesley volumes reached him from her. Thomas Jackson was a great collector of tracts, and he used to have them bound in sets of six, eight or ten. They have only recently been properly catalogued, and range in date from 1600 to 1850, but most of them fall between 1750 and 1850. It will be recalled that Thomas Jackson was President in the fateful year 1849. He has left copies of all the 'Fly Sheets' behind him!

2. THE COLLEGE PORTRAITS

SYDNEY G. DIMOND, *Resident Tutor*, 1935-41

THE Dining Hall at Richmond is adorned by the oil paintings which hang on its walls, and by that we mean, not only that the pictures add beauty to the room, but that they bring out and interpret something of the glory of the College itself. They are a visible defence of the habit of our fathers which decreed that the good men who kept the faith here should be immortalized on canvas.

Pride of place must be given to the portrait of John Wesley by Thomas Horsley, of Sunderland, which has the following statement pasted on the back of the frame:

'This oil painting of the Rev. John Wesley, A.M., was taken from the life by Horsley of Green Street, B.P. [i.e. Bishop's] Wearmouth, during one of his last visits to Sunderland, at the house in Wm. Street, B.P. Wearmouth, of my grandfather, Robert Hutton, Esq.,—has been carefully preserved in the family ever since,—was presented to me, Charles Hutton Potts, by my mother, E. J. Potts, some years before her death, and is now presented by me (in remembrance of 3 happy years spent as a student at Richmond Institution during the years 1845 to 1848 inclusive) to the Wesleyan Methodist Conference as established by John Wesley, with the request that it may be placed in the Richmond Branch of the Theolog. [sic] Institution.

'The Chapel in the painting was taken from an engraving of the City Road Chapel in London, which appeared many years after the painting was done, in the Wesleyan Magazine, and was unfortunately added to the original painting by my Mother's concent [sic].

'Witness my hand this sixteenth day of July 1863,
CHARLES HUTTON POTTS.
'Newbus Grange, near Darlington.'

There is a controversy about this painting, which is dealt with by John Telford in his *Portraits of John Wesley*, and in an article by the Rev. F. F. Bretherton in the *W.H.S. Proceedings* for June, 1941.

The least satisfactory of all the portraits is at the same time an extremely interesting contemporary painting of John Wesley by his friend, Dr. Thomas Olave, Vicar of Mucking, in Essex, and usually called 'The Olave Portrait'. Dr. W. T. A. Barber published an account of the picture in the *Methodist Recorder* for August 9, 1923, with a copy of the curious rhymes pasted on the back of the frame. The Olave documents giving details of the history of the painting were discovered by three students in the gallery above 'Jacob's Ladder' in the old Library in 1924, and in May, 1925, Dr. C. Ryder Smith set out the whole story in the *Wesleyan Methodist Magazine*. Since the painting was restored by Mr. Murcott in 1936, the figure of Wesley stands out clearly as he preaches by a graveside, with the fine old village church among the trees in the background.

One of the most delicate and sensitive portraits in the Hall is that of Richard Treffry, Junior, a small oil painting of one who was neither a student nor a tutor at Richmond, and whose only connection with Hoxton was that his father was appointed Governor there in 1838, the year in which Treffry, Junior, died, at the early age of thirty-one, after fourteen years in the ministry. Some authority attaches to the opinion that this portrait may be the work of Sir Thomas Lawrence. It has the purity of colouring which Lawrence achieved and which has a curiously hard effect, as if the colour had been laid on china. By contrast, the painting of Treffry, Senior, inscribed 'Rev. Richard Treffry, Governor of Hoxton, 1838–41', is in the grand style, rugged and full of strength, and reminiscent of one of the portraits of Sir Walter Scott.

Although Joseph Benson died in 1821, his portrait is rightly in our gallery because he belongs to the ranks of the early Methodist scholars. He was one of Wesley's itinerant preachers. He entered the ministry in 1771, and shares with Dr. Adam Clarke and Joseph Sutcliffe the distinction of having written commentaries on the whole of the Bible. The portrait is rather stiff and formal and belongs to the period when bituminous brown was the conventional colour for landscape and portrait backgrounds, but otherwise it might be that of a Methodist preacher or a Scottish elder.

With the portrait of John Farrar, Tutor, 1843–59, we come to one who directly links the earlier training of the ministry with Richmond, for before he was appointed to Richmond he was Governor of Abney House from 1839–43. He left Richmond to become Governor of Headingley, and shares with Thomas Jackson and George Osborn the honour of having been twice elected President of Conference. From above the clock (presented to the College by Dr. Barber), Mr. Farrar's portrait seems to survey the Dining Hall with a shrewd and kindly air.

In addition to a smaller oil painting of Thomas Jackson, the first Theological Tutor, in the Church History Lecture Room, there is a fine portrait of Jackson in the Dining Hall, presented by his students. Gracious and benign, with a certain majesty on his bearing, his portrait reveals something of the gifts and grace which made Thomas Jackson master in his own realm as a teacher of divinity and a defender of the faith.

Singularly graceful is the portrait of John Dury Geden. It was presented to the College by his niece, Miss Margaret

Geden, and belongs to the tradition which made portraiture a field for powerful work in British art. In the same class is the portrait of Alfred Barrett, Governor, 1858-67, presented by his daughter Agnes. A certain Victorian elegance seems to belong to the period, but there is nothing bland or conventional, and the beauty of feature and colouring in no way disguises the strength of character which marks this classic portrait.

More rugged and to that degree more vital is the picture of Daniel Sanderson. Here the painter has seized upon the great qualities of mind and heart which enabled Sanderson to govern the College during the whole of the time that it was owned by the Missionary Society and used exclusively for the training of missionaries, and for a further six years after the College was handed back to the Theological Institution. A whimsical touch of humour adds to the strength and tenderness which mark the man who from this canvas still seems to dominate the Dining Hall.

The portrait of William Fiddian Moulton has the merits and defects of being a photograph on canvas painted in oils by an artist. It has the qualities of a photograph without the interpretation of character which the master portrait painter can convey. An odd technical fault appears every few years in that the film on the canvas tends to peel off at some point and needs careful restoration. Fred Robins (the College engineer, who should be immortalized somewhere in this volume)[1] remarked that Dr. Moulton reminded him of Mr. Pickwick, and the portrait certainly has a good-humoured pontifical air, enhanced by the spectacles, which is definitely Pickwickian.

The portrait of J. Agar Beet is also a painted photograph and has the same technical defects as that of Moulton, but it is not so good as a portrait. The dome of the forehead is impressive, but there is a stiff primness, not unlike that of John Stuart Mill as painted by G. F. Watts, but the vitality is lacking.

In the Principal's Lecture Room there is a photograph of Alfred S. Geden, who was the son of John Dury Geden, and

[1] See p. 151.

was Tutor in Biblical Literature and Classics, 1891–1915.

We are happy in having on loan from the Rev. Dr. J. Alexander Findlay the very fine portrait of his father, inscribed: 'Presented to the Rev. G. G. Findlay, D.D., by his students at Headingley College, 1881–1902.' The painter was Arthur T. Nowell. He was Dr. Wiseman's brother-in-law, and painted portraits of a number of Wesleyan worthies. Nowell has on this canvas captured the spirit of the teacher and the saint, and the picture is worthy of the greatest of our portrait painters. Not quite so pleasing is the picture of the leader of last century's Forward Movement in Methodism. It is inscribed: 'Hugh Price Hughes, M.A., Student at Richmond College, 1864–7. President of Conference, 1888. This portrait was presented by his wife and family.' The form and feature of Hughes are set forth clearly enough, with something of his aggressiveness and a hint of humour, but perhaps no painter could put on canvas the flame of holy passion which was Hughes.

Three brass tablets in the Dining Hall commemorate Alfred Barrett, W. F. Moulton, and Benjamin Hellier. In one of the Lecture Rooms is a small oil painting of Jabez Bunting, but it is almost a miniature and gives no hint of the driving power which enabled him to be the founder and first President of the Theological Institution and at the same time Senior Secretary of the Wesleyan Missionary Society. Two marble busts in the Theological Lecture Room portray George Osborn and Thomas Jackson. The sculptor was John Adams-Acton, who often exhibited at the Royal Academy, and both are virile and lifelike. In the same room is a rather faded oil painting inscribed: 'Rev. George Osborn, presented by his daughter, Mrs. Strutt. November, 1926.' It is unfortunate that, with the exception of Nowell's portrait of Findlay, none of the oil paintings has the signature of the artist.[1]

The Lycett Room has an engraved copy of Mr. Frank Salisbury's portrait of Wesley, inscribed: 'John Wesley.

---

[1] If the College were in our hands, it might have been possible to take them out of the frames to see if any signature is concealed by the gilt slip, but that is impossible at present.

RICHMOND COLLEGE 59

b. 1703. *d.* 1791. H. Macbeth Raeburn Sct. Painted by Frank Salisbury. Portrait painted to commemorate the Consummation of the Union of the Methodist Churches, 21st September, 1932, from the authentic bust by Enoch Wood. Presented by the Artist to Wesley House Museum, 20th September, 1934. Exhibited at the Royal Academy, 1934.' This was given to the College by Edmund Lamplough. In the Staff Room is a small oil painting representing the landing on one of the Australasian islands of the Rev. John Waterhouse, who arrived there early in 1839. He is seen standing up in the boat, wearing a frock coat and silk hat, while his wife is being carried ashore by a stalwart native, a crowd meanwhile assembling on the beach to welcome the missionaries.

Framed photographs continue our portrait gallery in the Theological Lecture Room. One steel engraving, a period piece, is of the Rev. William Morley Punshon. The recent destruction of the Punshon Memorial Church at Bournemouth by enemy action may have reminded readers of the fame of one of Methodism's great orators. A photograph from the same period is that of Charles Garrett. Thomas Jackson's successor was John Lomas, whose portrait is inscribed: 'Rev. John Lomas. Born 1798. Died 1877. President of Conference 1853. Theological Tutor of this College 1861–68.' David Hill, one of Richmond's greatest sons and a representative of the missionary spirit of the College, would be a student under Lomas. There is an odd contradiction on the two tablets on the portrait, which read: 'Rev. David Hill. China 1864–96' and 'Student at Richmond College 1861–4. China 1865–95'. A typically Victorian portrait is that of the Rev. Joseph Sutcliffe, who died in 1856 in the seventieth year of his ministry.

The latest portraits are examples of photography at its best. The portrait of George Fletcher possesses something of the character of a Watts painting, so forthright and sincere is the expression. There is a life-size studio picture of W. T. Davison, which is the gift of some of his old students, and the photograph of Dr. Barber is on the same scale. Finally, we have, presented by old students, the portraits of the

Rev. Thomas Barratt, and of Dr. Ryder Smith. Mr. Barratt is remembered as perhaps the most beloved of Governors, and Dr. Ryder Smith as one through whom theology became the living Word. It is said that Mr. Barratt never grew up and Dr. Ryder Smith never grew old. Both were prophets of God to us, and of both stories are told that will be the delight of many generations.

Although they vary in aesthetic value and in historical interest, these portraits which hang upon our walls are symbols of our spiritual inheritance in the great Christian tradition of prayer and learning and friendship which is the glory of Richmond.

III. DOWN THE YEARS

SIXTY YEARS AGO

(1) A. J. NORMAN, 1883-85

ONE of my impressions of the Richmond of sixty years ago was the Spartan conditions of life there. Perhaps they were intended to prepare us for hardships abroad!—for in those days every man went to the foreign field. The monitor came round to our studies at six o'clock in the winter's morning to see that we were all at work. Friday was the weekly fast day, when no meat was put on the table. There was a ten-minute 'break' midway between the 7.30 breakfast and the two o'clock dinner, in which dry bread and water might be had by hungry students. We sat on wooden forms in the Dining Room; the tea-cups were an odd lot of assorted sizes, picked up at a sale. The rules were that no man might go outside the grounds after tea, even to post a letter; and on no account might a bus or train be used on Sunday. I have repeatedly walked into London and back to preach, and looked enviously at the passing buses when I was ready to drop with fatigue. The Governor, who had been a great missionary and walked vast distances on the Indian plains when there were no railways, still believed that if a student was not in good health, better than doctor's medicine was a long tramp to a distant village on the next Sunday! Indeed, men were afraid to let it be known that they were not well, as the cure would inevitably be an appointment at Hook, Halliford or Esher.

My old friend John Wesley Davis and I have had many a laugh over our first Sunday's experiences. He was to preach at Wimbledon and I at Merton. In the morning a senior student kindly piloted us a mile or two on the way, between the Penn ponds and through the Park. The good people who gave the students 2s. 6d. for their day's services naturally wanted it to be fully earned, so they asked me, though I had to go a mile to dinner and back again for tea, to address the

School in the afternoon. At the close of the evening service was the prayer meeting, and the mile again for supper before starting on the long walk home. My hosts accompanied me to Wimbledon, where I picked up Davis. By this time it was very dark, and we soon found we were off the path across the great Common. There was nothing for it but to get back to the lights of Wimbledon town, and start afresh. In time we came to the Robin Hood Gate of the Park, which was locked, and the gate-keeper gone to bed. After knocking him up, and listening to his advice about people keeping reasonable hours, our troubles really gegan. A thick autumn fog had settled in the Park. How many mistakes we made, or how we got to the College at last, as the clocks were striking twelve, I don't know.

The place was in darkness. We timidly rang the bell, and the Governor came. Before letting us in, and holding the door in his hand, he addressed us on the unpardonable offence of being about the streets at twelve o'clock on a Sunday night, and said that men could have no proper idea of the seriousness of the Christian ministry who acted in this way during the first week of preparation! When at last we got inside, I asked if it was possible to get something to eat, and was told: 'In the morning—at breakfast!' As I dragged myself upstairs, and bathed my swollen and throbbing feet, I wondered if this was a fair sample of a student's life! There was reason in the two local shoemenders coming up to the College every Monday night after tea. They always took away a sackful of Sunday casualties, sorely needing repair!

Speaking of the primitive conditions at Richmond sixty years ago, mention should be made of the little field of rough grass on which the donkey grazed, and where we attempted to play cricket during the short summer afternoons. It had never been levelled or mown, and sometimes the fast bowling of lusty young fellows flew about rather dangerously. One Thursday, William Spink had to preach in the College Chapel that evening, and his friends urged him to come out for a game and put the worrying service out of his mind. He was our wicket-keeper, and took his place behind the stumps. Soon a fast ball jumped up unexpectedly and hit him full in the eye! After bathing the injured part, a bump as large as a hen's egg formed, and the eye was completely closed. It was plain that preaching was impossible, and we went to tell the Governor. The old gentleman *was* wild! He could not understand men preparing for the serious work of the ministry playing at such a brutal and heathenish game; but to do so, instead of praying, before preaching . . .!

One of the features of Richmond sixty years ago was its fervent missionary spirit. This was natural, for every man was expecting to go abroad, and might any day be sent to fill a vacancy in Sierra Leone or Calcutta. Letters were read at table from old students who were with us a year before, and whose ordination we had attended. In those days it was improper to express preference for a particular field of work, or to hesitate about going anywhere, excepting only West Africa, which after our recent grievous losses there was known as the 'White Man's Grave'. Of my little year of only twelve men, five were asked to go to the West Coast, and of these, three—Clegg, Roe, and Bartrop lie out there.

Perhaps more should have been done by the College authorities to prepare the men for the entirely different conditions of life abroad. They might have been told something about tropical medicines, about customs and religious beliefs in the various fields, about learning languages, and school management. But as no one knew to what part of the world he would be sent, it is difficult to see what provision could have been made.

I felt at the time, and am of the same opinion to-day, that, with the vastly increased knowledge and the changing religious thought of the Victorian Age, our College ought to have had the most competent theological teaching. Too often the Theological Tutor was some elderly minister who had served the Church well in other departments, but whose views on all subjects were formed before Biblical criticism or modern science had appeared above the horizon. A theory of verbal inspiration of the Scriptures made most modern questions irreverent.

But the students of sixty years ago had read something of

the theory of evolution, the composite character of the Pentateuch, and what lies at the back of the Gospels. They had read Farrar's *Eternal Hope* and Cox's *Salvator Mundi*, and found it difficult to believe in the never-ending punishment for the sins of this present life. They were troubled about the creation of the Universe in seven days, and a crowd of its attested and seemingly unnecessary miracles in a world ruled by law. These questions were never mentioned from the theological chair; either they had not been heard of or the doctrine of verbal inspiration proved them untrue. But the long-since-ended battle with Calvinism was fought over again, and the old paladins set up and duly knocked over; the eternal Sonship of Christ properly insisted on; the views of Arius severely condemned, and the doctrine of the Second Advent made abundantly clear.

But it must not be thought that the colleges of the Victorian Age were merely museums of antiquities. The Assistant Tutor, W. T. A. Barber, and, after him, J. G. Tasker, put in hard work at geography and arithmetic, grammar and elementary science, which the young fellows surely ought to have learned before going there.[1] With the Sub-tutors immersed in literary subjects, it followed that practically all that bore directly on preparation for our missionary career and subsequent work in circuits at home fell on W. T. Davison.

He was in the early enthusiasm of his distinguished career. We owed everything to him, so admired and feared him; he was Richmond. We all greatly respected him, yet we never knew him. But on one Sunday night when I happened to walk back to College with him through the Park, for the first and only time I had a look into the real Davison, and found that he knew what it was to be a soldier in the hard-pressed fight for faith. When we met in class on Paul's Epistles on the Tuesday, he was the old Tutor again—arm's-length away; the window was closed. But I had had that glimpse.

Davison did much for us students. Could he have done one important thing more, and so made Methodism his

[1] The general low level of educational opportunities at this date must be borne in mind.—ED.

debtor? Thirty years later, James Moulton was staying with me, and as we walked over the hills he said: 'Davison has failed us. He ought to have led us into the new positions made certain by criticism and science, and frankly accepted by Anglicans and Presbyterians because they were evidently true. He had adequate knowledge, gifts of exposition and persuasive speech; our people trusted him and would have followed him. But in the critical hour he sat on the fence.' To which I replied: 'Davison belonged to an age when the fence was a prohibited area. The man who got us as far as the fence, sat on it and told us of the rich lands on the other side, was a veritable explorer and path-finder. Because Davison was sagacious enough to sit on the fence, your Ballard and Jackson, Ryder Smith and Wright and countless others have been able, without opposition or question, to cross over to the great inheritance beyond in the twentieth century.'

(2) W. H. Hart, 1884–6

This contribution is really a glimpse into antiquity. My day at Richmond is rather distant, and I hope to be forgiven if some of the 'impressions' should appear a trifle hazy when seen through the mists of all but three score years!

One of my earliest impressions was that the strikingly handsome exterior of the building was hardly matched by the convenience and comfort of the interior. But we were not there either for criticism or for comfort, and we settled down quietly and happily. The improvements made in later years to meet modern conditions could hardly have been expected then. There was a harmless pleasantry of our own by which 'Seven Dials' was the name given to one of the wings and 'Saints' Rest' to the other. I may modestly say that my 'den' was in the latter. Whether it was named as a tribute to the character of those who dwelt there, or because it was so close to the Governor's study that we had to live a quiet life, I will not venture to say. I remember occasional trouble when a few athletic 'Saints' went forth to endeavour to reform their brethren of the 'Dials'.

Richmond in '84 was still exclusively a missionary College,

but in '85 this was, happily, altered, to the advantage of the work and the closer sympathy, as the years passed, of men at home and abroad. At the time of our entry there was, through some earlier miscalculation, such a shortage of available men that we were told we could not hope for more than a two years' term. Things did not fall out quite so badly, but very few of the '84 men got a third year. Work had to be planned accordingly, but it was not good for the tasks of the years ahead.

The relations between the Staff and the students were not then quite as those of to-day. There was then a certain aloofness and an air of reserve on the part of the Tutors, which appears to have greatly changed. They were ready and willing to give help and guidance apart from their lectures, but they were approached with something akin to awe. There appears to be an atmosphere of brotherliness and comradeship to-day which did not then exist. There was, perhaps, on the part of the Staff rather more of the schoolmaster and less of the fellow searcher than there is now.

Our Theological Tutor was the venerable Dr. George Osborn, who, after the storm that culminated in '49 and the tragic years that followed, found a peaceful refuge at Richmond. His day was near its close, and there was too great a distance between him and his students. His theology was emphatically orthodox, and his ways antique in the extreme. He persisted, for instance, at the devotional opening of his lecture hours, in giving out the hymn two lines at a time! As most of us were quite well able to read, this seemed to us somewhat superfluous, and sadly bothered Bateson, our Precentor. In the next year, the Chair was filled by Joseph Agar Beet, and the change was startling. Dr. Osborn once did me an unforgotten service. When my turn came to take the week-night service in the old College Chapel, the Doctor was present, and I went to him the next morning. The text had been: 'Prove all things; hold fast that which is good.' At the service I felt a happy liberty, and enlarged on the duty and necessity of thinking for ourselves, and so forth. Though I thought I had a good time, the Doctor did not. Far otherwise! I had taken a dangerous line, and he spent about half an hour in showing me how. Both matter and manner were wrong, and to say that we should 'go in' for something or other was 'the language of the prize-ring, and not of the pulpit'. Then he walked me round the playing-field and back again to his house, and, not unkindly, said: 'When you preach that sermon again, remember what I have told you.' Disillusioned, and with an unfeigned humility of spirit, I replied: 'I don't think, Doctor, I ever shall preach it again!' He closed the interview by saying, with equal sincerity and powerful emphasis: '*I hope you never will!*'

Looking back on those days, one feels that, while we had on the whole the training necessary for our great task, there was too much precious time given to subjects which really called for a few months of purely preparatory work on more general lines. There was no regular opportunity for this preparatory period.

There was a definitely high standard of devotional life and experience set before us, though we often felt ourselves failing to reach it. The Governor's class meeting was helpful. Dr. Tasker exercised a very gracious influence upon the men, and we had some special seasons of great value to most of us. And the evangelical efforts of the students, of which we now read in a modern form, were anticipated by our 'Bands'. These were groups of five or six men, one of whom was 'bishop', giving one long afternoon a week to intensive, house-to-house visitation in certain localities—real home mission work; then a cup of tea with some of our own folk, and a long tramp home again.

It is full time for me to close, with much unrecorded. The life at Richmond was a happy one. True, we were under restrictions which no longer exist and which somewhat vexed the older brethren. Our field sports were almost wholly among ourselves, though a game with another College occasionally came off; and there were other matters concerning which there is greater freedom to-day. I don't think the men are now required to 'consult the Governor' about some things as they were then, and perhaps they are none the worse for the change. Richmond meant great opportunities to all of us, and to some like myself, who had come from business life, it was a new world of life and thought. Richmond threw wide open a door through which its sons have now passed for a hundred years, to carry (many of them to the ends of the earth), by the grace of God, the story of Christ and His Cross, and all the transforming message of His redeeming love. And that grace has been abundantly given for the work and the witness. Richmond men have no need to be ashamed of the Gospel of Christ. Far and near, they have proved it to be the power of God unto salvation.

A RICHMOND 'LOG'

George Jackson, 1885–7

I FIRST saw Richmond College at the 'July Examination' in 1885. At the ensuing Conference I was accepted as a candidate for the ministry, and in September entered the college as a student. After only two years, I was placed on the President's List of Reserve, and forthwith sent out into the work of a circuit. Such memories, therefore, as I can contribute are limited to the years 1885–7. They are of (1) the Staff, (2) my fellow students, and (3) the general life and work of the College. I have before me as I write the lists of Richmond students for 1884, 1885, and 1886—of all the men, that is, for there was no third year, who were my immediate contemporaries. But these, alas! are all the written records which I possess. Still, however mistaken some of my judgements may be thought, I am not, I think, seriously 'out' in my facts.

I

The College Staff in 1885 consisted of Daniel Sanderson (the Governor), J. A. Beet, W. T. Davison, J. G. Tasker, and F. W. Kellett (the Assistant Tutor). Kellett was himself an '85 candidate. A brilliant Cambridge student, he stood, in matters of scholarship, head and shoulders above the rest of us, while his lovely and lovable character, despite the overmastering nervousness of which he was the victim, endeared him to everybody. The Tasker of those days I hardly had a chance to know, as I was not a member of any of his classes. But I think I am not wrong in saying that he was more successful than any of his colleagues in establishing easy and personal relations with the general body of the students. My own outstanding memory of him is of occasional addresses delivered on the old quarterly 'Fast Day', and at the opening of a new college year. In particular, I remember some of his shrewd counsels to the freshman who had been a big man in a small circuit. Of Daniel Sanderson I would rather not speak. Good and kind a man as he was, God never meant him to be a college governor. Yet the blame for his appointment should in fairness be laid not so much upon himself as upon those who were responsible for making it. There are uses in this world for round pegs, but when we make them into plugs for square holes, there is certain to be trouble. As a circuit minister and missionary advocate—Sanderson had spent many years in India—he might have done good service, but as governor of a college he was a very round peg in a very square hole.

The 'star' of our Staff—if such a term may be pardoned, —was, of course, Davison. He had a mind of quite extraordinary fineness and delicacy, of which his own finely chiselled features were the fitting reflex. As a teacher he was superb, and it is hardly possible to exaggerate the debt of successive generations of students to him. But—I hope 'Davy's' old admirers will forgive the 'but'—there were two serious limitations to his influence. One was his inability to enter into the average man's mind and put him at ease with him. I imagine that Davison himself knew this, and probably regretted it as much as any of us. The other, I think, was deliberate and cultivated: I mean, his fencing attitude, his unwillingness to declare his own mind in face of the difficulties which the studies of the classroom inevitably raised for us. There is involved in this the whole conception of the duty of the teacher to the taught, and this, of course, cannot be discussed here. I will only say that, according to my reading of the facts, if candour has slain its thousands, the lack of it has slain its ten thousands; and it was this lack in Davison that, at least for some of us, was fatal to his supreme influence as a Christian teacher, deep and far-reaching as nevertheless it was.

It was just at this point that Beet, who entered Richmond as a Tutor at the same time that I entered it as a student, did me such timely and lasting service. I was then both very young and very ignorant, and much teased by foolish questions through which only a man of Beet's engaging frankness and simplicity could have helped me to find my way. I have often wondered since what would have befallen me had I been confronted with the harsh, unbending theology of his predecessor, George Osborn. Beet had little of Davison's genius as a teacher. Compared with him, indeed, he must sometimes have seemed little more than an awkward and clumsy amateur. He had, moreover, certain little and oft-repeated oddities of speech which provided endless mirth for the college supper table. But the transparent sincerity and goodness of the man, his high courage and devotion to duty —one example which I had from his own lips remains with me as the most precious of all my college memories— triumphed over everything and won for him a way to the hearts of all who came really to know him.

II

From the Staff, I turn to my fellow students. If I have counted right, my two years at Richmond brought me into contact with just over ninety of them. When I entered college, twenty-seven were already in residence. My own year contributed another thirty-four, while the freshmen of the following year numbered thirty-one: ninety-two in all. Of these in April, 1943, only twenty-six still remained in the *Minutes of Conference*, all of them supernumeraries. Of the rest, a few have left our Communion; the others have been claimed by death.

Two points relating to the years 1885–7 may be mentioned. From 1868 till then, Richmond had been used exclusively as a college for men who had already been designated for work abroad. But in 1885 a new policy was adopted, with the result that seven of that year's students—myself among them —were for work at home. At the same time the experiment was made of bringing coloured students from West Africa to be trained side by side with our own men. Two came in '85 and another two the following year. But the results were not judged encouraging, and the practice was afterwards discontinued.[1]

'Not many wise, not many mighty' was Paul's comment as his eye ran over the faces of his Corinthian converts; and much the same might be said of the Richmond students of 1885-7. Kellett was the only man amongst us with any pretence to scholarship; we produced no future Presidents of Conference. Parkes Cadman achieved something like international fame, but not till long after he had ceased to be a Methodist. Yet if, as a whole, we can claim little more than a respectable mediocrity, on the other hand there is little in the record to put us to shame; and after all, perhaps, the world owes as much to the many with two talents as to the few with five. As one glances over these faded college lists, now nearly sixty years old, it is with a glow of thankfulness, and even of pride, that he recalls the long, faithful, unforgotten service, at home and abroad, of which they still speak. There are other things, too, not to be spoken of here —things too intimate, too sacred for comment, friendships which first took root within those old college walls, which grew with the years, and still remain among the most real and enriching of all the things which God has prepared for those who love Him and love one another.

III

It is natural, I suppose, that in a brief retrospect such as this persons should be the first to catch the eye. But, besides reminiscences, I am asked to contribute something in the way of what the Editor calls 'critical estimation'. On his shoulders, therefore, be the responsibility for the paragraphs which follow.

[1] But has now been revived.—ED.

Allowing for the differences in the point of view of the 1880's and the 1940's, there were some gaps in the Richmond curriculum of sixty years ago which I find it very hard to explain. For example, I left college in 1887 without ever having so much as heard of 'The Problem of the Old Testament'. Not a whisper had reached us in our closely-guarded walls of the controversy which for a whole decade had been raging in Scotland around the head of Robertson Smith. What seems still more inexplicable, and, indeed, hardly credible, is that during the whole of my two years I was never in a class of which Christ and the Gospels were the subject of study. Lectures on 'Systematic Theology', of course, there were—two or three of them every week—but the New Testament seemed to be regarded mainly as a textbook in Greek, the Old Testament as a textbook in Hebrew. We crawled over a few chapters in each of them at the rate at which beginners in a difficult language might be expected to move; but of the Bible as a whole, of the English Bible, of the Book which was to be the basis of all my future ministry, I was almost as ignorant when I left the College as when I entered it. I am speaking, it should be understood, of and for myself alone. How far other men's experience tallies with my own I do not know. I was, I remember, reading for the London Arts degree at the time, and I was excused some classes in order that I might concentrate on my work for it; but neither this nor anything else seems a quite adequate explanation of the facts I have named.

Most lamentable of all was the so-called 'class meeting' which met weekly under the leadership of the Governor. What should have been the peak of the week's experience was for many of us its nadir, so ghastly in its unreality was it. The Governor had before him a list of our names, and calling upon one and another to speak, as he thought best, he ticked them off as he did so. The result was that men went to the meeting with something of a 'speech' in their heads, in case they should be called on, fired it off if they were, comforting themselves with the thought that, with so large a class, their turn was not likely to come again until many weeks were passed. 'The pity of it, Iago! O! Iago, the pity of it, Iago!'

Finally, to bring these fault-finding paragraphs to a close, the right relations between Staff and students had yet to be discovered and established. We saw our tutors in the classroom; we saw them hardly anywhere else. Our personal ties with them were, as a rule, of the slenderest. In the whole of my time at Richmond I was only once invited to a meal in a Tutor's house. These are not pleasant things to dwell upon; they belonged, I suppose, to the traditions of a day which has now passed away, and it may seem ungracious to recall them. Nor should I have done so had it not been that the points I have named are just those at which the judgement of a later generation has wrought the most decisive change, and so by implication has justified the criticisms which I have ventured to make.

But this is not the note on which I should wish these memories to end. Whatever was wanting in them—and of this I have been a good deal more conscious since than I was at the time—my Richmond experiences will always remain a big item in the balance sheet of my life. I entered college a penniless youth—my mother was a widow with a large and young family and I could ask nothing from her. Yet my Church, with a generous trustfulness which probably no other Church in the world would have shown to an untried youth, provided me with tuition and board for two whole years without the cost to me of a single penny. How, again, can I estimate the worth of those outlooks over a wider world, which came to me through daily contact with Tutors and students, and in the frequent week-end visits to the churches and homes of our Methodist people? It was thanks largely to these things that I was able—not then, indeed, but at a later time—to pass through the revolution in men's thoughts of the Bible to which my generation was born without danger to my faith in Jesus as Lord. For this, as for much else which I only half realize myself, and which it is certainly impossible to tabulate, I shall always be among the most grateful of Richmond's sons.

FIFTY YEARS AGO

E. Stanley Edwards, 1892–5

Fifty years ago the standard of theological education was not quite what it is to-day. A few graduates came for a year's course, and they may have found the year a little dull. The rest of us were rather ordinary fellows, very anxious to learn all we could in our three years.

But the friendships we made fifty years ago were as true and precious as friendships ever could be. They did not depend on constant intercourse, for very soon we were half a world away from one another. And they didn't always depend on correspondence; for the early days of a missionary's life, pegging away at the vernacular, in tropical heat, didn't encourage correspondence. And there were some times more desperate reasons. Romilly Ingram, after a year at Richmond, went out to India in 1894. Two years afterwards he died of confluent smallpox; he had caught it while visiting one of his Hindu High School boys. We heard afterwards how all night long a stream of Indian lads had passed through the room where the poor disfigured body lay, and how, later, the little bits of broken white marble which had been strown over his grave were taken away as sacred relics by these lads. There are old men to-day to whom his friendship has been one of God's greatest gifts in long lives. And there are other College friendships which have gone on and deepened for fifty years, with very little correspondence, and only occasional meetings. But as we look back we know that it was these friendships that made College life so precious.

And yet how much we owed to the Staff of the College. Others have written of them in these pages; I may mention them in passing. I think of 'Daddy Fletcher', the Governor. As I look back it seems to me that there was a very healthy spirit in the College in his days. I never heard a smutty joke all my three years; and I never knew a serious quarrel. Then there was Agar Beet, our Theological Tutor. Peake puts his commentary on *Romans* in a list of six specially recommended. His teaching was, some of us felt, all too matter-of-fact and clear-cut. There was no touch of imagination; no suggestion of the mystery of truth. But there was a good foundation for further study. Turning to A. S. Geden, I feel that his lectures on Comparative Religion were the only subjects in the curriculum which had any specific bearing on our work as missionaries. I remember that Mrs. Geden was a great help in the life of the College. She had a beautiful voice, and many of us carried away very happy memories of musical moments spent in her home. All the Staff were accessible and friendly to the men; and I think we all felt that we were very welcome in the houses of the Tutors—an intimacy which was, perhaps, strongest in Geden's house. Mrs. Fletcher was an invalid, and used to be wheeled about the grounds by Mr. Fletcher; we all knew her and loved her, and admired her patience and cheerfulness.

The A.T. in our time was Thomas Stephenson. He contributed considerably to the interest of College life by becoming engaged to Miss Fletcher. There was a touch of novelty and romance in our somewhat ascetic life in having a Tutor in love with the Governor's daughter.

There was, of course, a great deal of enthusiasm about anything connected with foreign missions. Well-known missionaries on furlough would come and talk to us. There was Owen Watkins, with his stories of work in the Transvaal. Of a very different type was Dr. Barber, with his unforgetable 'Come with me, and I will show you . . .' and in a moment we were in China, rubbing shoulders with strange folk, and seeing into their hearts too. And there was Dr. Ebenezer Jenkins, one of the last of the old-fashioned Methodist preachers, with his clear-cut features, white stock, and precise way of speaking. But it is his addresses at the quarterly fasts that remain in the minds of many of us. I remember still the amazement with which I heard him say that he was still tempted to sin, and still had a hard fight with evil. I was just beginning the conflict, and it was a strange comfort to find I was in such company.

There are other things at Richmond that went to make up the many-tinted web of College life. There were the visits of friends, and tea with them in one's study, with some of Lotze's delicious cakes. Lotze the confectioner, whose shop was, conveniently, just outside the upper gates, was a wiser man than the unfortunate brewer who, years before (according to a very well-known tradition), hearing that there was to be a college here, built a public-house opposite one of the gates—and learned, too late, that the men were all teetotallers!

But there is no doubt that the week-ends at Richmond had most to do with our general health. As a rule we were out preaching every Sunday, and in the homes where we stayed we were treated more as old friends than as strangers. It was there that we began to find out, what was to become one of the great joys of our life, the warmth and reality of Methodist hospitality. Some of the appointments were rather an ordeal —Brixton Hill was one of these. Dr. Rigg might be sitting in the dim light under the deep gallery; or, just in front of you, in the middle of the congregation, you might see the Rev. Fred W. Macdonald with his family. That was enough to test the nerve (or was it the grace?) of the coolest man, though there never was a kinder hearer than F. W. M. And again and again we should find a minister in the vestry after the service to say a word of encouragement or appreciation that always made one feel desperately ashamed. I think those who had no word but one of criticism, didn't come into the vestry!

And there were other Sundays when we were not out preaching, when we used to go off, generally in couples, to hear some great preacher in London. Dr. Parker was at the City Temple in those days, and we found that he spoke to our hearts as few others could. And there was always Hugh Price Hughes in the evening at St. James's Hall. There was a standing invitation to any Richmond man who went to that service to go straight into the vestry before the service and, when Mr. Hughes came in, to go with him on to the platform, where there was a seat for him. It was a characteristically kind thing to do, for the Hall was invariably packed, and we should never have got in otherwise. There were some who said that he was not a great preacher; but we knew they were wrong. Whatever his subject was, he brought us to Christ. And when the service was over there were always men and women going into the Enquiry Room, and he always asked us to go too, and help them to find Christ. It was not easy for us youngsters, for you met all sorts of people there. But it was a great and searching opportunity, and we learned a great deal from it.

Later in the evening we should be back in College with the others. Some had been preaching. 'Any conversions?' they would be asked. Some had been listening, and had come back full of a great experience. On the table were great jugs of milk or cocoa, and cottage loaves and cheese. We sat round the fire talking. To-morrow there were classes again, and the blessed routine of learning. But we had been out in the world, to which, some day, we were to take the Master's Gospel. We were not fit yet; but we had learned something more of its need; something more of our own need. We must work harder while we had the opportunity. And there were those other sheep, not of this land; we must be ready when the time came to take the Gospel to them. So week-end and Sunday we must prepare. How much we owed to those teachers of ours! How much we owed Methodism! How much we owed the Master! Fifty years ago! And we have never paid the debt yet.

FORTY YEARS AGO

Arthur Walters, 1898–1901

My first and never-to-be-forgotten recollection of Richmond 'forty years' ago' (to be quite accurate, it is forty-five years) was when, having duly passed the District Synod, I presented myself at the July Committee then held at the College. I was well primed in the theological textbooks of the day, to say nothing of 'proof texts' (I could have proved anything), and felt it would take a clever examiner to floor me, though I had already received a nasty jolt at the Synod by being asked, 'How many children had John Wesley?' I wondered what that had to do with theology. I see now that it has quite a lot. On my confidently replying thirteen, the Synod seemed surprised and not a little amused.

I had previously visited the College, but this was a visit with a purpose. As I walked its spacious corridors, climbed its steep ascents, glanced at what then seemed to me its huge classrooms, sniffed a certain scent which from that day I have always associated with Richmond, wandered round its glorious grounds, I began hopefully to picture myself as one of its students. I remember with what awe I looked at the members of the Committee—indeed, with reverence, for reverence had not then wholly passed out of life. They were all much-travelled ministers, clad in clerical frock-coats, and not a few had beards or whiskers. All were very kind—though, I thought, a little patronizing.

One of my most vivid recollections of its personnel was the minister in charge of the candidates, Peter Thompson—a great, burly man known throughout Methodism for his mission work in East London! Blessed be his memory! Well, the miracle happened, and I was accepted. Whilst at the Committee I had formed a friendship with a fellow candidate which has proved lifelong. We were the two youngest candidates of that year. He has since attained considerable eminence in the theological world. Great was my joy when I found we were both designated for Richmond. He was a lively, versatile youth, caring little for authority, but careful not to offend it. We soon fixed on adjoining 'dens', and bedrooms in the tower, the idea of this being that we might be away from authority, and we had discovered that, although gas was turned off at night in some sections of the building, it was on all night in the tower. May we be forgiven for this youthful scheming. These were the days before the luxury of electric light and central heating. For heating, each den had its coal-box filled once a week, but by a visit to the coal dump one could always replenish this. The students kindled their own fires, and each was supplied with an arrangement for drawing the flames. My friend and I would take it in turns that, as soon as the morning bell rang (an unearthly hour), one crept downstairs and lit the fires. With the help of the blower both would be blazing long before we came down. Happy days! No fuel control then!

Ours was a small year. Few remain to tell the tale. George Fletcher, the Governor, used to speak of us as 'a select few'. I do not know to this day what was in his mind. He was given to cryptic sayings. He was a man of great seriousness, seldom smiling, to say nothing of laughing. But when he did smile, his whole face would light up and radiate the kindliest feeling. He spoke in a very quiet voice, and as he was the Governor we did not like to suggest that we could not hear him. Perhaps he was at his best in the weekly class meeting, for he spoke out of a long and rich experience. He would call on each by name. This was always something of a nightmare to me, and I think to others; but however feeble and halting one's words, he invariably replied in response, 'I am glad you have said that, Mr. So-and-so,' or 'That is a very important point!' This greatly cheered me, and I have always remembered it in class meetings which through the years I have been called on to conduct.

The sermon preached on a week-night in the College Chapel by the students, and followed by a criticism class, was an event which loomed large in our lives. How critical we were of each other! (I mean in the study.) May Heaven forgive us! The Governor had a favourite phrase which applied to not a few sermons—'somewhat sketchy and superficial'. No preaching in his eyes was worth anything unless it contained some exposition. What would he have said of some of the sermons preached to-day, when not a few seem at pains to expound everything and everybody save the Bible and its writers—Wells, Shaw, Joad, and others of their class; this ism and that ism!

Theology was taught with no uncertain voice. Dogmatism had not wholly passed. We had not in those days so feebly acquiesced with the scientists or tamely bowed the head to the psychologists. We still held a bit of ground of our own. Agar Beet, the Theological Tutor, was a distinguished scholar who had published several books in high regard—not the least, a Commentary on *Romans*. He had a way of speaking of 'my *Romans*' as if it were the last word to be said. We loved him for this. It was so refreshing. He was lively, vivacious, humorous (often without knowing it), childlike, and sometimes bland, never dull. Although regarded by some as an advanced (even dangerous) thinker, he was among the most orthodox of the orthodox as orthodoxy is accounted to-day. I owe him much and bless his lively memory.

Church history was taught by the Governor, but we had far too little of it, and he lacked the gift of making it a live and fascinating study. I feel that this was a big miss in my education. He was also responsible for lectures on Pastoral Theology and Preaching. Few, alas! took these very seriously, and they dealt chiefly with sermon construction. What good it would have done some of us to have had a course on how to talk to the young, or on 'Children's Addresses'! I would have courses on this in every college, with a criticism class made up of long-suffering children.

Hebrew and Greek were taught by A. S. Geden. Shy, unassuming, speaking little above a whisper, he could at times make the poor student feel very small. But he was a great encourager of effort; down on the slackers, but merciful to the triers. I picture him leaving the College Villa carrying a great pile of books. Other subjects (it was a very limited syllabus in those days) were taught by Thomas Stephenson. One always felt that he had a great reserve of learning and scholarship. All my remembrance of him is happy. I received at his hands consideration I little deserved.

Looking back on the lectures and teaching, I have the feeling that not enough pressure was brought to bear upon the men to work. Individual oversight was lacking. Many only got the merest smattering of things. This was especially true of many who came with little or no education. It was easy by wise cramming to do quite creditably in the examinations, but how much knowledge had one made part of oneself? I am glad to think that these weak points have been strengthened through the years, and are still a matter of earnest consideration for the authorities.

It was in 1901 that the College produced its first *printed* magazine. I had the honour of being its first editor.[1] It was

[1] P. 154.

really rather a tame production. The truth is that print made us a bit shy. We were afraid to let ourselves go.

Students were much in demand for Sunday appointments, not a few donning on these occasions clerical frock-coat and silk hat or clerical hat. The student would indeed look *somebody* as he set off on Saturday with his little black bag and umbrella. We all carried umbrellas. It was at this period that a few bold spirits started wearing a clerical stock—at that time looked on with some suspicion. Others compromised on their Sunday attire and wore a black or white bow, looking like waiters off duty. Others looked as if they were just off to get married, so gay was their attire. Indeed, Richmond Station saw some strange sights on Saturday afternoons.

It was a small world in which we lived. This is one of the things I marvel at when I look back. A very small world! Tremendous events were happening outside, as they are always happening for those who have the eyes to see; but we were unmoved, living our little lives in our little world—very conscious of our importance. I suppose this is inevitable in such a community.

Now may an old man, or at any rate one rapidly growing old, end by giving a word of advice to those just starting on the way? College gives to a man a priceless opportunity. How few realize it, seize it, use it to the full! I write as one of the many who failed to do so.

THIRTY YEARS AGO

LESLIE D. WEATHERHEAD, 1913-15

IT has been a delightful relaxation to me in busy days to obey the Editor's injunction and try to throw my mind back thirty years to the day when I entered Richmond College. I set off from my home in Leicester in company with a man who was returning for his third year. It was kind of him to take a freshman under his wing, and much of that strange shyness which every boy knows on setting off for his new school was overcome by this kindly act. But he made one great mistake.

He took me up the drive from Friar's Stile Road and in at the side entrance. Even if it had meant a detour he should have brought me in at the Queen's Road entrance, or, at any rate, from the side drive should have led me round to the front of the college. When, at a later period, I have shown people Richmond I have always taken care that their first impression should be a front view of that glorious building. To those who are proud to belong to her, as many of us reading this book are, that first impression of her beauty and stately grandeur will never be forgotten. I am familiar with all the other theological colleges of our great Church, but I don't think any reasonable person can deny that Richmond is far and away the most impressive building.

Led in by the side door, I was shown my first study in Upper Chequers. The windows are rather small, and creeper hung down over them, obscuring the little light there was, and I remember Gordon Early, the Chairman of the College in 1913, saying in his cheerful voice, in answer to my comment, 'It seems rather dark', 'Oh, you will get used to it.' Early then took me up to my bedroom, which also seemed rather a bleak affair. There were just the rough wooden boards with one mat, a chest of drawers, a washstand and an iron hospital bed. Comfortable enough, but certainly not luxurious.

What happy days they were! Each began by a thump on bedroom door and a message. If the awakener were Gordon Early, cultured and rather pious, it was a polite, 'Time to get up!' and, as he passed down the corridor, I can remember him singing the verse:

> *'Dark and cheerless is the morn*
> *Unaccompanied by Thee.'*

Other knockers-up were not so considerate. They would bash on the door, and then open it and leave it open, allowing a stream of cold air to rush through the room, shouting meanwhile some such message as, 'Show a leg, you lazy buffers!' Then followed prayers taken by one of our own number in turn, and always an ordeal. The men wanted their breakfast and were impatient of long prayers and very critical. Anything in the nature of 'side' came in for scathing criticism afterwards, and some of those who led the prayers could not escape the temptation to endeavour to make an impression. I remember one prayer which began, 'O Lord, Thou knowest that each of us before Thee has heavenly possibilities and hellish propensities.' Whatever else the prayer contained nobody knew, for all were concerned in stifling their laughter.

The meals at Richmond were good and I must not take space in describing them because in these days they would make the mouth water. There followed a morning of lectures, an afternoon of sport—football or tennis or rowing or walking—an evening of study, a most satisfying supper and then either more study, or college meetings, or a chat in one another's 'dens'. What could be more attractive to a boy of nineteen (my age when I entered college) so pleasantly to be allowed to prepare for what he considered the greatest vocation in the world?

The professors in my day were a mixed bag. The Principal was dear old Dr. Davison, with white side-whiskers which he ruffled up with both hands when anybody gave a stupid answer, smiling benignantly when we gave what we knew was the answer he wanted to hear. I still have the notes I took of his lectures and not infrequently refer to them. I shall always regard it as a very great privilege to have been under his guidance in forming a foundation of theological reading. In my second year I was Chairman of the year, and in my third year Chairman of the College and had frequent contact with 'Davy'. I found him to be strangely lonely, and when, impulsively, I asked him on leaving if I could have his photograph, he signed one and gave it to me, and rather pathetically added, 'I wonder if any of the other men would care to have a copy?' I secured half a dozen and he seemed so pleased to be assured of the respect and affection in which he was held.

Dr. Geden tried to teach us Hebrew. His knowledge was immense. His power of imparting it almost nil. All that he said could afterwards be read in his own books on the subject. I am sure he was a man of deep piety and vast learning.

In my day the Governor of the College was T. H. Barratt, a great soul and a great saint. Frankly, I was rather frightened of him in my first two years, and only really got to know him when I was brought into daily touch with him on the business of the College. I remember that he used to take the Friday night class meeting, and that once when we were all bowing in prayer F. W. Townsend, my college chum (and still my dear friend), nudged me and said, 'Look at Barratt!' He was kneeling in prayer, his eyes wide open, looking up at the ceiling, but with such a rapt expression upon his face that a feeling of awe came over us as we looked at him. Afterwards Townsend said, 'What did Barratt remind you of?' and I answered immediately with the answer that was in his own mind, 'The face of "Christ in Gethsemane" in Hoffman's picture.' 'Tim', or 'the Guvvy', was and is one of the most Christlike men I have ever known. Some of the passages from his lectures on Homiletics come back to me now. Thus: 'Every sermon should contain at least one idea'; or, 'Get on with your job and don't try to climb the Connexional ladder'; 'It is treachery to the Kingdom to do things on Saturday'—and then in a very incisive voice—'*or eat anything*, which will impair your fitness to serve God on Sunday.'

Harry Bisseker taught Greek and Psychology in my day. I find it difficult to speak of him because I owe him so much. It was he who first kindled in my mind an interest in psychology which has been my hobby study for the last thirty years. I fear that I have not with the same avidity pursued my studies of the Greek Testament, but that is not the fault of his teaching. His is a gentle and most lovable personality, and in my time we felt it was a great privilege to have him.

The Assistant Tutor thirty years ago was Conrad Skinner. I think we were most proud of him, not because of his gifts of scholarship, but because he had been cox of the Cambridge boat. We used to sit on the floor in his room right up in the tower, supposedly to read Shakespeare or study logic or tinker with Greek verbs, but the naughty boys amongst us used to make desperate efforts to steer him off his course and get him talking about other matters. He was too good a cox for us to be able to interfere altogether with his steering, but sometimes, as it were, we could stop rowing and the boat would drift into easy conversations about current affairs or Cambridge memories. He had a most brilliant literary gift, and if he gave the time to it, would, in my opinion, be one of the most famous novelists in England. The novels he has written in my view are in a class of excellence by themselves.

It gives me very much pleasure to realize that I have kept in touch with practically all the men in my own year. They might object to their names being mentioned, but I hold them in loving remembrance still as my dear friends. From time to time, if they have half a Sunday free, they turn up at the City Temple, and I find I can pick up the friendship, though I have not seen the friend for over a score of years, and together we can recall some brilliant sally made at 'Seats'.[1] Surely the Methodist ministry must be the most wonderful brotherhood in the world.

If the Editor gave me unlimited space, I should love to recall in detail some of the 'den' teas we had. On Friday afternoon we were allowed to have tea in our studies and invite friends either from within or without the College. People who had pretty sisters had a popularity not entirely their own, and we used to sit down to the most amazing feasts. Tinned salmon would be followed by tinned peaches and cream buns, and then all the dirty 'pots' would be pushed on one side and we would gather round a roaring fire (none of your electric radiators in my day), bring out immense pipes and smoke and yarn until it was time for the Friday class meeting. If fasting is a necessity of spiritual apprehension, it is a wonder that at a class meeting held after a 'den' tea spiritual things were ever spiritually discerned.

Yet those class meetings were memorable. T. H. Barratt's Communion addresses live in the memory still. I never hear the hymn—

'My God, I love Thee—not because
I hope for heaven thereby'

[1] An informal meeting of the College held after each meal to discuss any necessary business. It provided an opportunity for the College wits to show their mettle.

without it carrying me back to a never-to-be-forgotten Communion talk by T. H. B.

In my day we were practically all engaged almost every week-end in preaching in the circuits of greater London. Our fees were all pooled after the expense of the journey had been deducted. The third year had three-sixths, the second year two-sixths, the first year one-sixth, divided amongst the men.[1] One preached in large chapels and small, in mission halls and country circuits. One stayed sometimes with the wealthy and sometimes with the poor—all of it a most useful training for those who seek to be all things to all men.

The athletic side of the college life was rather a marked feature in my day. I think they must have been hard up for men, because I remember playing half-back myself. We played Westminster College and usually beat them (I don't forget the mind's tendency to remember more easily the pleasant than the unpleasant!), and we played the great London hospitals and other colleges housed in London. Some of the men who came up to College had never been away from home before and apparently never played a game of football. One student, whose name I will not give away even for a substantial contribution to the City Temple Rebuilding Fund, and who is now a distinguished superintendent of an important circuit, turned out in football shorts the first afternoon he was in residence, but omitted to remove his long-legged pants first. At first we gazed in incredulous astonishment, thinking he was wearing some elastic bandage or other to strengthen his knee joints. When the truth was realized, the hoots of mirth made it impossible to go on with the game and the Rev. brother retired to the security of his bedroom and removed the offending garment. On his return to the field some one from the touch-line stole away to his bedroom, tied the pants to the halyard on the flagmast and pulled them to the top of the College flagstaff, where they floated gently in the autumnal breeze. Very gravely at 'Seats' that evening the Chairman of the College requested Mr. —— to remove his underwear from the flagstaff and to

[1] The division has been equal, irrespective of year, for some time now. —Ed.

promise not to use the said flagstaff again for laundry purposes.

The games played on the first year men during the nights of the first week they came were a great tradition which I hope has not now passed away. It seemed strange to me at the recent Conference in Birmingham to look down upon the bald head of the chairman of a district and recall the day when he was visited in his bedroom, during the first week of residence at Richmond, by a group of hideously disguised second- and third-year men and requested without delay to stand up on his bed and sing a solo. On his refusing to do so, he was taken by force in his pyjamas on to the top of the tower, and locked on its roof, with nothing between him and the stars, until he consented to sing at least one verse of a self-chosen solo. It also gives me some satisfaction to recall another chairman of a district who for some offence, imagined or real, was condemned by the Chairman of the College to go back to his study using the fire-escape ladder, which we used to keep near the fives court, instead of using the stairs. When half-way up the ladder, buckets of water were thrown on him from the roof and the fire-hose brought to bear upon him from below. Wet and wretched, the unfortunate district-chairman-to-be could not retreat, for the fire-hose met him from the bottom, but had to struggle up rung by rung, clinging tightly lest the force of the fire-buckets emptied on him from the roof shook him from his grip. I do hope that students of the future will carry on these traditions and will not allow budding Methodist preachers to be deprived of these important aids to the education of a Methodist minister!

I was the last College Chairman before the Great War closed it against us. It was a sad chapter and, in spite of our training for the ministry, we came as near hating Dr. H. B. Workman as doesn't matter. This was not so much due to any flaw in his character as that he was the Principal of Westminster College, and, by some unfortunate twist of affairs, Richmond was not closed for military occupation,[1] but to allow Westminster men to come in, their own college

[1] But for Westminster's occupation, it would probably have been.—ED.

having been commandeered. We took this as a great grievance. Some of us, myself included, were sent out into circuit, and the other men were divided between Handsworth and Headingley, obviously very inferior places of ecclesiastical training.

So my own experiences of Richmond ended with the war that we thought was to end war, and now there is another upon us, during which once more the dear old place has been not only closed, but damaged by the bombs of the enemy. Yet it is grand to think that Richmond lives on in the hearts of men who knew her and loved her and who still find it an inspiration to try to be worthy of her traditions. May she soon be re-opened and her grand traditions be continued in the lives and ministries of her Methodist sons of future years.

TWENTY YEARS AGO

Frank B. Roberts, 1920-2

The phrase 'twenty years ago' marks the beginning of a new era, rather than an exact date. For five years Richmond had been closed as a theological college. War had scattered her sons to the four corners of the earth; some had gone into circuit and others into the Forces. During those five years other voices had taught in her lecture-rooms, and other students gathered within her walls. In October, 1920, she began a new lease of life.

No college began with more diverse elements. There were men from Didsbury and Handsworth in equal numbers; others had spent some time in circuit or the Forces; while a few had been accepted as candidates at the Conference of that year. Those of us who had come from the other colleges wondered according to what principle we had been chosen. Those we had left behind had no doubt about the reason! The intellectual cream of Methodism's youth had been left in the Midlands and the North. On the other hand, those who had been transferred were confident that the authorities intended the new College to start with men of light and leading. The tutors who had sent us on our way, being men of discernment, had long since noted the zealous students who lapped up learning as dogs lapped water, and had set us by ourselves to dwell in the land of Richmond. Probably neither of these views is correct; rather, the Providence of God had cast us together in the same age and place, that we might kindly help each other on.

Certainly we had much in common. Most of us had been in the Forces or on war-work. Our lot had been cast among all sorts and conditions of men. The common gibe about a minister knowing nothing about life as it really is did not apply to this new Richmond. A great many of us had looked death in the face on the battlefield; some bore the scars of war upon body and mind. A few pursued their studies not unacquainted with pain through wounds received in war. Our brethren who came from circuit life let us know they were *the* men. They did not appreciate being called juniors by those who had some experience of College life. The latter made the senior year, and all others were juniors for the first year after re-opening. However, these things became of little consequence in the deep fellowship which grew up among us.

These were the men who had to weld themselves into a unity which should be worthy of old Richmond. The task was no easy one. There were customs and traditions of the earlier Richmond with which our newer and more recent ones would have to accord. Certain old customs we swept ruthlessly away; for others we had scant respect; but we were not 'lewd fellows of the baser sort'. How could we be, when the Missionary Honour Board was on the College threshold to haunt us with the valour of our forebears? Nor were we unacquainted with the story of those who had gone, who had made our College loved and honoured throughout the Church. And was there not a memorial unveiled in our day to those who would have been with us, but had fallen in battle? No! we did not forget our fathers and history, or the *noblesse oblige* of loyalty; but those things did not efface the peculiar characteristics of the new generation of students.

If the task were great, we were not daunted. We had the high hopes and courage of youth, and the generous support and interest of our Tutors. No relations could be happier than were ours with those who had to train us. They trusted us, and put us on our honour. Authority was wielded, but it did not rob us of friendliness or the opportunity of approaching them about any question or problem which might be troubling us. No rule or custom was continued because it was old. The test was always its use and value.

A great concession made to the new generation was the permission to smoke in the study. What our Fathers in Israel would have thought about the gift will not bear contemplation. It is rumoured, however, that those sons of a saintly Victorian age who were supposed to love the hair shirt also loved the pipe. There were stories of these austere brethren lying on their backs in the study, with noble heads well up the chimney, puffing fragrant smoke from a pipe as votive offering to my Lady Nicotine. The new rule had wisdom in it, though the smokers did not enter into their new estate at once; for more than half of us were non-smokers. An anti-smokers' society was formed, which fought a valiant rear-guard action. One day a raid was made on the smokers' dens, and pipes were seized with the intention of burning these idols. The attempt proved abortive, as a warning was given and the foe had a chance to bury his treasure. This war went on for many weeks amidst much fun and banter, till the *coup de grâce* was delivered by T. H. Baker, who placed on the notice board a large placard bearing the words, 'Praise the Lord upon the pipe'! No one bothered about his somewhat free rendering and exegesis. Such is the way of propagandists in every generation. From that day smokers and anti-smokers dwelt together in peace.

Let no man think we were pampered by the College staff. Consideration was given and tolerant regard shown to many of our suggestions and requests, but in certain matters the reins were held very tightly. Pre-war Richmond made many conquests in the world of sport, and we intended to keep the trophies which had a place round the walls of our venerable old building. To this end, we began to mould and train new teams out of a group of men who had never played together, but who were expected to make sure those cups and shields should remain with us. Money for sports outfits was found, but not a minute off from a lecture was allowed, be the match ever so important. When time off from lectures was refused for a match, we looked upon our professors as veritable Rehoboams who would allow this Shishak of a mere lecture to take away the treasure of the house. The learning they desired to give us was accounted the mere substitution of tawdry brass for gold shields. Fervour was stirred, and we knew ere long the battle would be joined. This came when an important game had to be played in connection with a cricket shield. We approached the Tutor concerned, telling him a certain train must be caught to get to the place of play at the time appointed. Could the players be excused his lecture? He told us: 'The lecture will be cancelled.' We were about to let up a whoop of triumph, when he continued: 'We will take it to-morrow afternoon instead'! This was ignominious defeat, and somehow we had to rationalize this set back in order to maintain our sense of importance. We concluded that our beloved Tutors thought us a lot of lawless ex-Service men who needed plenty of work and discipline. This attitude of ours had all the injustice of youth, though it did not go beyond a mood of impatience which soon passed away. It was not realized, and no one pointed out to us, that circumstances in Methodism were such that no more than three years at College could be given, and only intensive study could get the course of work set out for us covered. Moreover, as a theological institution, a certain standard had to be maintained to give us the status with London University which we desired. This meant some men must work for degrees and others sit for the Certificate of Religious Knowledge, and before long Richmond students would have to work for the Diploma of Theology. Therefore, even if it had been desirable, it was not possible for the Staff to 'let up' the least little bit.

In no lecture-room was seriousness and high purpose absent, but humour from the desk often pointed a moral and adorned a tale. At times the habits of speech and mind of our instructors provided merriment. Who will ever forget the answer when the dogmatism of youth demanded a categorical reply to a question which touched the world of imponderable things? 'The answer to that, Mr. —— is both and neither!' or 'To that I should say, "Yes"—and "No"!' How my generation loved to gird at the habit of the Assistant Tutor of bringing reference books innumerable into the room! The great pile of ancient tomes men placed on his table before he came in never seemed to cure the habit. And, be the subject psychology or ethics, shall we ever cease to remember how, with tense expectancy, we waited for the shaft of humour or the apposite remark from another Tutor. It always came before the lecture was over. After the shot was fired there was a few moments' pause, then his face became wreathed in smiles, his knees shot up with a jerk, and a rapid movement was made with the hands as he gleefully rubbed his knees! Only those who witnessed this can know the delicious delight it gave us. Again, a Greek class was taken on a certain occasion by a Tutor who did not usually teach Greek—one whom we all honoured for his long and faithful service in a well-known Methodist school. On the morning in question, he asked a certain man to begin translation. When he had finished he called out, 'Next boy!' Then another—'Next boy!' This went on all through the hour, and although the suppressed merriment threatened to explode in laughter, the 'next boy' continued to be called upon.

While Richmond was closed during the last war, our premises were occupied by Westminster College. When the time came for them to move out, they inadvertently took our piano with them, but they left us a central heating system. The piano in due course came back, but I suspect that nothing would have induced them to relieve us of the heating system. This contraption was a good illustration of the difference between fact and theory, of blue print and finished product. This mark of progress was supposed to save labour and fuel as well as give heat and comfort. Whatever else it did, the heat and comfort were missing. In the winter months the College was a veritable Arctic region. To make matters worse, the first winters after reopening seemed exceptionally cold and closed up not only the hand of man, but every kindly and generous emotion towards those who had the thing installed. It robbed us of fireside chats and made private study a cold and shivering business. A chorus of grumbles and complaints was raised, but that did not heat the pipes, and the only fire we enjoyed was the one in the lounge, where we congregated in our free time.

But the stars in their courses fought on our behalf. On Saturday, November 26, 1921, a few students decided to invite some ladies to tea. These men sallied out to do the necessary shopping. The day was dull and cold, and sombre reflections filled their minds. They had invited friends to tea, but a cold, forbidding grate was going to spoil everything. Suddenly the door opened; Sangster had returned from one of his excursions with a parcel. He must have looked like one of the gods, for as he unfolded the bulky package we thought he must have been in touch with Prometheus. Our eyes feasted upon wood and coal! We did not stop to consider whether some modern Zeus would seize him and allow eagles to consume his liver; our chief concern was to let him apply the useful art of lighting a fire! What a party we had! The warmth and good cheer of that fire set the mind free from its frozen bondage. Many a new joke was told and glorious pun was shaped. There was not only good food, but a feast of mind and flow of soul.

One swallow does not make a summer, nor a single fire give warmth to every study, but our fire was strangely prophetic of things to come. During that evening, when most of the men were out, our harmless frivolity was disturbed by H. T. Proctor, who came running to tell us there was a fire in the Lounge. As we ran along the corridor, we seized a Minimax fire extinguisher. Reaching the scene of the fire, we mounted the steps leading to the gallery. Some valuable books were removed and the Minimax and pails of water quickly ended the conflagration. On Monday instructions were given to light fires in every study, and so for a brief season we told around the glowing embers all we felt and all we saw. Told of the things we planned and purposed.

Spoke of the deep things of the Faith. The experts ended these happy days by diagnosing the cause of the trouble to be a faulty flue, but the experts did not solve the problem of a heating system which would not heat. I believe a later Richmond overcame this difficulty.

I have tried to tell the story of my Alma Mater as I knew her. To recapture the spirit and impart it to others by a few selected incidents from the abundant and rich life of those years. Much must be left out for want of space and much more because some things can never be told. The men of twenty years ago went out to a difficult world—to work not free from disappointment, but also of some conquests for Him whom they serve. If any of us has done anything worth while it is because he had the honour of being a Richmond man. Until the mists fall and the eyes grow dim in this world —yes, and after—every one of her sons of twenty years ago will thank God he had a place within her sacred walls, and was of her fellowship.

A TUTOR'S MEMORIES

T. H. BARRATT, *Resident Tutor*, 1915-16

To no man living is it given to write the history of Richmond College. Of all the unknown hundreds of its sons, each has his own peculiar memories and his own particular point of view; for each the vast majority of those who came and went before him are but as names, and those who are to follow, for him, have no existence. But the greatest things which go to make up 'Richmond' are for us all a common treasure.

I have been asked to say something of my own memories of Richmond and of its tutors and its men. Possibly my chief memory is of the astonished shock with which I received a certain telegram from Conference in July, 1909. The man who sent it was an old schoolfellow, and not without a sense of humour; but next morning's post brought a pile of letters which left it beyond a doubt that Conference, which I had never attended since my ordination eleven years before, had appointed me, without the slightest warning, 'House Governor of Richmond College'. I recalled the words attributed to Dinsdale Young that 'the essential qualifications for a College Governor were that he should be, like Eli, old and heavy', in both of which essentials I was conspicuously lacking. Of Richmond College I knew nothing, save from the dubious position of an examiner in Greek. In the year 1909 'Principals' and 'Resident Tutors' were alike unknown; Conference had made a man still in his thirties 'Governor'. All the world wondered, but no one more than I.

However, there was nothing for it but to obey, and in a fortnight's time my wife and I were at the College, having tea under the famous mulberry-tree with my predecessor, the Rev. George Fletcher. For him it must have been a trying and painful day; he had been Governor at Richmond for eighteen years, and now he had to hand over his house and his position to one whom he had only known as a chubby little boy at Woodhouse Grove when he himself was Governor there. But he showed us all around the place, answered all our questions, and was kindness itself to both of us. His memory is cherished and respected by all who had the privilege to come within his influence.

Early in September came the students. The situation was at first peculiar and embarrassing. The new Governor was mistaken for a student, and by at least one third-year brother was, with some emphasis, treated accordingly until he was seen to be preparing to take evening prayers from the Governor's chair in Hall. Next day came the first 'Tutors' Meeting', at which the Governor always took the chair; my first and only act in that capacity was to propose that Dr. Davison should be requested to preside at every meeting of the Staff throughout the College year. At the following Conference (1910) the position was made more regular; Dr. Davison became 'Principal' and I was 'Resident Tutor'. So ended the long line of College Governors. Dr. Davison had won my reverence and affection when he was my tutor in theology at Handsworth. For some seven years at Richmond we shared each day our common duties, and in the midst of them, we shared as well our common sorrows. He was very good to me. The other members of the staff were J. A. Vanes and A. S. Geden. F. Bertram Clogg was, as Assistant Tutor, a tower of strength in all that concerned the welfare of the College, with which, to its great benefit, he has been ever since connected, save for an interval of some eight years, due to war and other circumstances. The second A.T. in my time was Conrad Skinner, now in his twenty-third year as Chaplain of the Leys, and famous in his time as cox of the Cambridge boat for three successive years. The third of my A.T.s came also from the Leys, but, to their lasting loss, the students never knew Will Dyson. The College was almost empty when he came, for it was in the second year of the war, and Dyson held a commission in the Gloucesters, who were encamped across the Park. He used to come to our Communions and our class meetings, and it was always late when he and I walked together towards Roehampton Gate.

To know him was to love him, for a more tender, brave and humorous soul never wore a soldier's uniform. One night, 'somewhere in France', Dyson was ordered to 'fetch a prisoner' (soldiers will understand). He took a few men with him and in the silent darkness they crept towards the German trench. But when they were but a few yards off he ordered his men to stop, and he went on alone. His one idea must have been to get his prisoner 'without hurting anybody'. He crawled up, put his head over the top of the trench and whispered to an astonished German soldier, '*Kommen Sie hier!*' The fascinated man actually was beginning to 'come here', when an officer lifted his rifle—and Dyson only lived for twenty minutes. An English Tommy who loved him had, unknown to Dyson, crawled up the trench behind him. The man seized his legs in a vain attempt to rescue him. They were both made prisoners. In after days that unknown Tommy told us that all Will Dyson said to him was: 'Say something cheerful, old man. Say something cheerful!' So passed the last of the A.T.s I knew at Richmond.

It was in the autumn of '14 that the storm burst upon our College as it did on all the world. One morning in September

I met in the corridor a first-year man in the full uniform of the London Scottish. He quietly remarked: 'I'm off, sir. I had my training in Pekin during the Boxer troubles, and I've got my orders. I shall be all right, sir. I know God will look after me.' Before Christmas he was a scout in no-man's-land and for eighteen months he was never touched. But one morning he awoke in the city of Cork in Ireland, with two nuns watching over him. To this day he has not the slightest idea how he got there. Other men soon joined up too. When conscription came, theological students were exempt, and each man was at perfect liberty to do what he himself thought right. The students asked permission to be drilled in the field by an Army sergeant and to have the use of the butts. The tutors gave leave to any who desired it, on condition that each man's freedom was respected.

The end came in the autumn of 1915. The few of us who still survived were sent elsewhere and our College was for five years in other hands. In 1919 some eighty students, demobilized from the Army, had to be cared for, and no College was able to receive them excepting Didsbury, which for some years had been a hospital. And thither was I sent, unwilling, by the high authorities, far from the College I had learned to love.

These lines are being written on May Day, 1943. Of Richmond's hundred years, more than a third have passed since first it was my home. The men I knew as students are growing elderly and wise. Where are they all this morning? It so happens that I have their record. The number of the men with me at Richmond was 176. Of these no less than 130 are in our ministry to-day, either at home or overseas. Of the remaining forty-six, ten went back to South Africa, whence they came to us for training, seven are in the Church of England, ten are in other callings, and nineteen have already entered on that Higher Service for which the oldest of us is still but a probationer.

Time and space would fail me to tell of those whose names I fain would mention. And the men it was my privilege to know at Richmond are but a fraction of a mighty army. The generations follow one another all too quickly in our College life; we all become immersed in other interests and other duties, until we may become to one another but as memories and names. But 'the City of God remaineth', and the glimpse we caught at College of fellowship and brotherhood is after all but a foretaste of the things to come. 'We shall know each other better when the mists have rolled away.' Meanwhile we can but seek to serve our generation according to the will of God and our manifold diversities of gifts; until we enter on that Higher Ministry where His servants do Him service with added powers and deeper knowledge, because His Name is on their foreheads and deep within their hearts. 'Man is not MAN as yet', and it doth not yet appear what we—even we—shall be. The work of Richmond is only just beginning. *Sursum corda.*

IV. THE TUTORS AND THE STUDIES

THE TUTORS

FRANK CUMBERS, 1927-31

AMONG the occupations current since Mother Eve's indiscretion made work an almost inescapable necessity, there are some which seem to the uninitiated pleasant, simple, and restful. Among these is the office of 'College Tutor'. Sometimes to men labouring in circuits there comes the feeling that these are not as other men. 'A prominent Methodist personage' once said to Alfred Barrett: 'Surely the duties of the Governorship at Richmond must be of a very light character?' Mr. Thomas Barratt's words in the Didsbury Centenary volume[1] give a fitting answer to these stray rankling thoughts: 'If at an earlier stage of his career he should have been the manager of an hotel, a doctor, a lawyer . . . a gardener or estate manager, a plumber or a decorator, a specialist on drainage, heating apparatus, cookery and kitchens—on almost anything, his knowledge will come in very handy.'

At Richmond's opening, the Staff consisted of Thomas Jackson (Theological Tutor), John Farrar (Classical Tutor), and Philip C. Turner (House Governor). Chief stress was laid on theology and on pastoral oversight of the men. A junior minister was to teach other subjects, including arithmetic and grammar (an indication of the educational level). As the work developed, additional subjects tended to be left to the Classical Tutor. The Governor had also the responsibility for finance, premises, etc., all of which takes more time than some would think, though Joseph Entwisle, as Governor of Hoxton, had found time fairly regularly to attend John Hannah's theological lectures! Not until 1930 was the Governor (by that time 'Resident Tutor') relieved of the oversight of the College Chapel. A change was made in

[1] On p. 16.

1910, when Conference adopted the titles of 'Principal' and 'Resident Tutor' (see p. 95). Dr. Smith suspects that in the old days the Theological Tutor came off the lightest, but that duties outside the College, such as Connexional Committees, absorbed a good deal of his time.

George Fletcher wrote of *Thomas Jackson* (1843–61):[1] 'He was a very venerable and beautiful old man. The sight of him seemed an inspiration. His theological lectures practically ignored all but Puritan and Methodist theology. One of his favourite maxims was, "Whatever is new is not true, and whatever is true is not new", so that on the whole it was rather dry food and not stimulating to thought. But we venerated the old man, and enjoyed his preaching.' 'Who that was privileged to know him,' wrote George Osborn, 'can ever forget the cheerful smile, the greeting, the quiet humour which betokened a mind at ease, the love that overflowed on young and old!' His old age was eminently beautiful. His obituary notice, speaking with unusual candour, calls him 'a slow, plodding man. Even as a preacher he attained not only efficiency but distinction through careful exposition and whole-hearted devotion. He applied himself with all his heart to the improvement of such talents as were granted him, and with the Lord's pound he gained ten pounds.' George Osborn said that his powers of application seemed unlimited, so that what he read he made his own, and could give an account of a book he had read, years afterwards, as though he had just read it.

He did not lightly estimate his task. 'When I was bordering upon sixty years of age', he says, 'to be forced into an employment so onerous as that of Theological Tutor I felt to be unreasonable and a real hardship.' He seems to have become reconciled, for later we read: 'When my second Presidency[2] ended, I returned to my quiet course of life at Richmond with a satisfaction and thankfulness which no words can express.' Unfortunately, he had a serious failure in health during 1860, with alarming attacks of pain, and though his health was restored he never regained his strength.

The first Classical Tutor was *John Farrar* (1843–57), who

[1] *Eleusinian Magazine.*   [2] 1849.

had previously been Governor and Tutor at the Preparatory Branch at Abney House. George Osborn speaks of his modesty, humility, diligence, and courtesy. He followed his Richmond term with ten years at Woodhouse Grove, and when Headingley opened in 1868 he was appointed Governor there. From this source we have details which will stand equally for Richmond. He understood the art of governing by love, of making men trustworthy by trusting them. 'A quiet word from him, a single look, was enough to ensure order and compliance. He made the [Headingley] college not merely a place of instruction and discipline, but "a family of faith and love", the home of a Christian brotherhood.' He was as nearly the perfect Governor as well could be, with the art of ignoring trifles and reserving his strength for principles. 'The scrupulous neatness and perfect finish of his personal appearance was an analogue for the orderliness and finish of his mind. His stores of varied knowledge seemed never out of place, any more than the books in his carefully arranged study.'

Four men held the post of Governor in fairly quick succession. *Philip C. Turner* was the first (1843-6). Of him little is recorded. *W. W. Stamp* (1846-8) was known as a great administrator, and was President in 1860. *Samuel Jackson* (1848-55) has left a record of zeal for Methodist day schools and of love for children. He was before his times in advocating their special claims on the Church. *W. M. Harvard* (1855-8) brought an impressive record of missionary service which must have been a great inspiration to the young men in his charge. He had accompanied Coke to India in 1810, and had committed his body to the Indian Ocean; he had served in the Isle of France and Madagascar, and finally in Canada, where he was President of the Conference.

Farrar's successor as Classical Tutor was *Benjamin Hellier* (1857-68), himself a Richmond man, having entered in 1844. He was remembered as a shy student, diffident to awkwardness, and with a gravity beyond his years, and reserved. Others in the students' class meeting found him a great help. He went to Didsbury as Assistant Tutor, and all but six years of his ministry were in the colleges, first at

Richmond and then at Headingley. G. G. Findlay declared that Hellier gave Headingley its own ethos.

There was a wonderful unity and singleness of aim about him. When duty was ascertained, then without talk or question, obedience followed. That what was right must be done at once, was the axiom of his life. G. G. Findlay spoke of his rare lucidity of mind. Obscurity was his special aversion: 'Always make sure of your facts', was his constant dictum. He would never attempt to teach anything that he did not himself understand. In manner he was somewhat phlegmatic, deliberate, abstracted, blunt—even quaint—in speech. 'His mind moved slowly,' says George Fletcher, 'but there was a certain massiveness about him, with a touch of dry humour.'

He was a great Bible student, possessing a visual picture of the Greek Testament, and could wellnigh recite Romans from memory. As a preacher he was noted for his full and clear exposition. When on one occasion he preached in his home village, an old servant said afterwards: 'I did expect that Mr. Benjamin was come back a great man; but I did understand every word that he did tell about!' The attractive 'Life' written by his children reveals among other things how much a busy man can do for his children's education.

They have left us a picture of him walking in Richmond Park, reciting from *L'Allegro* Milton's description of the dawn. W. F. Moulton wrote of him: 'Mr. Hellier furnished as fine a type of Christian manliness as it has ever been my privilege to witness'.[1] He could be quietly severe; and in his restraint there was that which made his disapproval all the more painful. 'It was like a reproof from the lips of passionless rectitude.' He is recorded, though, as saying one morning in 'sermon criticism class': 'Well, brethren, it would not be wise to spend more time in criticizing the sermon of last night than the brother did in making it; and therefore we will go to our Rhetoric!'

Alfred Barrett (1858–68) followed Harvard as House

[1] See the remarkable testimony on p. 200, *The Path to Perfection* (Dr. W. E. Sangster).

Governor. Those who knew him as the quiet Tutor might never have dreamed that as a youth he had travelled a hard-riding 'circuit' in business over the whole North of England, that his ministry commenced in the slums, and that this was followed by a term of efficient debt-reducing at Great Queen Street (the predecessor of Kingsway). When made Governor, he stipulated that he should himself give lectures in Philosophy and Church History, the latter being his *métier*. Not content with these tasks, he led the students on crusade, and soon almost every village within walking distance had heard the cheerful voices, the praying, and the singing of the Richmond men. Soon ten or a dozen places appeared on a 'plan', with the Governor as superintendent of the 'circuit' until[1] substantial chapels were built, and a Richmond circuit formed much wider than the present one, with a minister in charge.

A hard student, he loved the theological deeps. He was a great preacher, with sermons remarkable for beauty of language, depth of thought, and the impressive energy with which they were delivered. He never preached without impressing his hearers with the conviction that they were listening to a man who lived in blessed communion with God. Those who knew him were aware of a constitutional tendency to depression, against which he fought constantly. Mighty labours as a young minister had aggravated this tendency and caused him intense suffering. He had a delicately poised nervous system, and felt things intensely, with resulting strain. Yet, knowing well the inevitable result, he drove himself hard. 'What he suffered from was overwork.'

With the passing of Thomas Jackson from the scene, there came as Theological Tutor *John Lomas* (1861–8). He had a great name as a pastor and visitor, and in thirty-five years' itinerancy had served but seven churches (a unique record for those days). Miss Anna Hellier has written of 'a shy, old-fashioned little gentleman with dim blue eyes and snow-white hair, witty and charming in congenial company, and a very fine preacher. He had a singularly clear voice, and was a master of beautiful English. A more unworldly man there

[1] Declares his son Howard, upon whose memoir we have drawn freely.

could not be, and he looked the saint he was.' Another[1] has spoken of the 'splendour of thought and diction quivering at intervals through his lectures, glorious as the pulses of the Northern Lights'. Hellier, speaking of his preaching, once declared that though but a schoolboy during Lomas's term in Bristol North (1839-42) he could distinctly remember some portion of every sermon he had preached. 'In prayer', said Dr. Stacey, 'he seemed at once to plant himself directly in front of the Throne and to draw his hearers after him, keeping them there until the close.'

When invited to Richmond, he doubted before he accepted, questioning his qualifications, though no one else did; and since he had been Headmaster of Kingswood when twenty-two, he need not have feared. His capacity for teaching and the charm of his personal influence were soon evident. His theology was Biblical rather than scholastic. In 1868 he moved to Headingley, and we have, preserved for us by a student there, a copy of some of the prayers he offered before lectures.[2] 'His teaching was as near perfection as it could be.' We should like room to quote the tribute of the President at his funeral.[3]

Lomas was succeeded by *George Osborn* (1868-85), who came from the secretarial chair at the Mission House. We discern two strains in the impressions men gained of him. On the one hand, we find a strong determination to maintain the old forms—to carry on the torch of Jabez Bunting (and men have carried worse torches): and on the other, there are testimonies to a quiet kindness and charm. Perhaps, like the rest of us, he was a bit of a mixture! His character was strong and definite; he was steeped in everything traditionally Wesleyan, conservative in every fibre, and averse to the new learning—lay representation and Bible revision being equally anathema! His father had spent an evening with Wesley, and everything early was sacred to him. 'He might have been a contemporary of Wesley's', said F. W. Macdonald, 'so minute was his knowledge of all that concerned the history

---

[1] Alfred Selby, *British Weekly*, February 10, 1898.
[2] *Methodist Magazine*, 1878, p. 291.
[3] *Ibid.*, 1878, p. 15.

and the writings of the founder of Methodism.' Of his mastery of Conference, his overwhelming knowledge of our standards, his unrivalled influence in the legal assemblies of Methodism almost from his probation, we could write much. Such things do not lead to personal popularity with the crowd, but never did a man care less for it.

So far, the picture will not prove attractive to some; yet we have ample testimony to his great powers. His utterances in Conference were not the dry-as-dust utterances of a Methodist lawyer; there was a mysterious, often overwhelming unction. He had an extraordinarily emotional vein under which Conference was often deeply moved, even if previously restive. He was always called upon to wind up the Conversation on the Work of God, and excelled in this. Further, we read of a rare geniality in private, a winsome manner which attracted children to him as if by magic.

It is not surprising that his lectures were little more than expositions of 'our standards', with skilful marshalling of their Biblical support.

Henry Haigh once wrote of the Doctor's kindness after his college sermon. 'You and I together ought to be able to preach very well,' said Osborn. 'I want you to write as many sermons as you can while in college. Leave a broad margin and let me see each sermon. I will annotate it in red ink.' It was the beginning of many other kindnesses, lasting far beyond college days.

Daniel Sanderson (1868–91) became House Governor in the 'clean sweep' of 1868. Every Richmond man knows his portrait, and will see reason in a letter written home by W. Gregory Harris while a student: 'The old Governor, the Rev. Daniel Sanderson, came in and read prayers. He is a peculiar-looking man with rather a cynical expression, in appearance rather like a Roman priest!' Yet those who knew him best spoke of him as 'sunny', 'frosty but kindly'—best beloved where best known. He had the reputation of a Spartan (there was a 'students' strike' in his time) but of kind-heartedness in trouble. Gregory Harris relates that, coming back late one night with friends from an Albert Hall concert (presumably by the time-honoured window), he encountered the

Governor. 'He didn't lecture us, but took us to his private apartments and gave us an excellent supper!'

He came to the exclusively missionary college with a great reputation for overseas service, and with a stock of missionary stories and experiences which amazed the men. He had cut the matrices for the first Kanarese types, and on one occasion assisted Whitehall with the translation of a document which had baffled all others.

He loved the open fresh air, and his greatest delight was an early-morning walk in the Park. He waged lifelong war with woman-kind against the encumbrance of curtains—unsuccessful everywhere except his study. Work was the breath of life to him, the more varied the better. It was said that he could make a pulpit and preach in it; translate the Bible into Kanarese, cast the type, print the sheets and bind them, go into the villages, collect a crowd of natives and preach to them in their own tongue. He built the mission house at Tumkur. His photographs, made in the early days of the art, when acids from England evaporated on the way out, when he had to dissolve half-sovereigns to get his gold chloride and cottonwool to get his gun-cotton and collodion,[1] were the wonder of his grandchildren.

He left the reputation of having managed the college at less expense than any other; but this hardly made for general popularity. His son was walking the dimly-lit corridor one evening with an old lady. 'The gas is poor to-night,' he said. 'It's not the gas!' she retorted. 'It's your stingy old father!' But he forgot economy when it came to giving away his own.

Turning to the third of the 1868 triumvirate, one despairs of describing *William Fiddian Moulton* (1868–74) in brief space. We might best say, 'He was the perfect Tutor', and pass on. His academic career was amazing. Matriculating at the earliest possible age (sixteen), taking his B.A. at nineteen, his M.A. at twenty-one, he was a scholar in the strictly technical and professional sense to a degree which no Methodist preacher had been before him.

To deal first with his work outside the colleges: he made his name by translating and annotating Winer's *Grammar of*

[1] *Methodist Recorder* at his death in 1902.

New Testament Greek. It was a revision which meant a virtual re-writing; traces can be found of his careful, conscientious, never-weary hand on almost every page; he made literally thousands of emendations. It was inevitable that when the Revision Company was selected, he should be included as the youngest of the twenty-six. Did space permit we should quote Westcott's tribute[1] to his work on the New Testament Revision, and its marginal references.

In Methodism he is counted as one of the great Presidents. 'Men were astonished' (why?) 'to discover that the self-suppressing scholar was a man of affairs, and an ideal moderator.'[2]

From the beginning as a Tutor he raised the level of ministerial training. 'Mr. Moulton soon made his presence felt', writes George Fletcher.[3] 'It was like increasing the pressure of steam in the working of machinery.' He persuaded Fletcher and four friends to rise at 4 a.m., to study for London Matriculation, and got them through it in six months.[4] 'He moved among us', said Henry Haigh, 'strong, great, and good, the knightly gentleman, the brilliant scholar, the enthusiastic tutor, the humble Christian and faithful minister.' The sixteen years at Richmond were the happiest period of his life. Among his pupils we record Hughes, Bowman, Stephenson, Haigh, and Hill.

His services to all the colleges and to ministerial training were very great indeed: he remodelled the examination system. It may be said that he began the transformation of the outlook at Richmond. Up to his time 'Methodist Theology' held pride of place. Jackson and Osborn were both masters in this sphere, and that of Methodist history. With Moulton was begun Biblical study in the modern sense of the term. He was interested too in social reform, and regarded the Leysian Mission as the essential corollary of his work at the famous School. Hugh Price Hughes found in his shy tutor a warm friend and stout supporter.

[1] Hurst, *History of Methodism*, p. 1419.
[2] Abel Stevens, *History of Methodism*.
[3] *Eleusinian Magazine*, 1901.
[4] See Selby's tribute, quoted by G. G. Findlay in his *Life*.

He founded the Leys School, and although this lies outside our scope, one story is revealing. Long after the establishment, a neighbour said: 'You know, Mrs. Moulton, when we heard that a dissenting school was coming to the Leys, we quite expected to have our windows broken!' Dr. Moulton was able to prevent such calamities! And his work left a profound impression on the University town, and afforded a new insight into Methodist character.

'The many-sided man often turns out to be slight and unimpressive on every side. But this is precisely what Dr. Moulton was not. Whatever he knew, he knew deeply and well; whatever he touched, he touched with a sure hand.'[1] Men said that he was made perfect in love. 'An unkind thing he could not say, an ungenerous thing he was never known to do', and when they called him 'the saintly scholar' they did him justice.

F. P. Napier (Classical Tutor, 1875–83, after three preliminary years as Assistant Tutor) has left little memorial, and subsequently left Methodism for the Church of England. He shared Biblical Literature and Classics with *G. G. Findlay*, who came the same year and taught at Richmond until 1881, when he went to Headingley, where they claim him for their own. But all the Colleges owe him much, for he was zealous in keeping the needs and opportunities of theological training before the Methodist public. He was one of the finest scholars of his generation, and one of the greatest teachers of his Church. His studies of Paul's Epistles are memorable, and so is his work on the history of Methodist missions, contained in three of the five volumes of that work. As a preacher, he was treasured by those who will look for something deeper than the superficial arts of oratory. There are many to whom his Communion addresses are among the most sacred memories of life.

A man of tireless industry, methodical even in his times of rest and recreation, he loved the open countryside and rejoiced in physical exertion. But he always returned to the study with zest. What he wrote he would revise and re-

[1] G. G. Findlay, *Methodist Magazine*, Vol. 93, p. 54.

revise and work over until the importunity of the publishers availed to stay his emending hand. He had a feeling for the just and apt in expression which amounted to a passion (and those who have worked under his sons will be quick to believe this). Slovenliness of expression and glibness of phrasing were alike impossible to him.

His life was little marked by outward change, and his adult life knew but two homes—Richmond and Headingley —and Headingley claimed thirty-eight years of that life. He wrote once: 'I learnt from my father, and in his person, to revere the Methodist ministry. I learned to love the Methodist people. Conference has made me a tutor to its young men. I have loved the work and lived for it.'

W. T. Davison came first to Richmond as Classical Tutor (1881-91). He went to Handsworth in 1891, and during those years he reached maturity. After thirteen years at Handsworth he was Connexional Editor for a year, returning to Richmond in 1905 and retired in 1920, having been Principal since 1910. He lived quietly in Richmond after his retirement, and died there on November 7, 1935.

Professor Clogg[1] says that his first memory of the Doctor was at July Committee, and suggests that no candidate ever forgot those few minutes. He had a remarkable gift of eliciting what a student *did* know. His scholarship won recognition for Richmond in the University, where he was Dean of the Faculty of Theology. Many regret that his published works do scant justice to his spirit and power, though they are far from undistinguished. Teaching, like others (notably Moulton and Findlay), in times when the spread of modern views was causing difficulty among Methodists, he encouraged his students in the new ways of thought.

Full tribute to his preaching is paid in the memorial volume.[2]

It was a Handsworth student who wrote: 'He was the best teacher I ever studied under; he kept admirable discipline. No one ever ventured to be inattentive in his classes, and the sight of that keen, intellectual face, so like Charles Kingsley's,

[1] *Old Chariot*, 1935.
[2] *Mystics and Poets*, W. T. Davison (Epworth Press).

was a rebuke to slackness and a spur to diligence. But my debt is greater than an intellectual one. I had been in his class for a month or two when I began to wonder whether I had really a religious foundation to stand on. Then I noticed how the Tutor's face lit up at prayer and at the name of Jesus, and I felt I could trust him to guide me.'[1]

He was a remarkable blend of quickness of temper, even irritability, and charming tenderness. His mind thought with the speed of lightning—often forked lightning. He gained respect and veneration—and sometimes fear, his severely disciplined mind was intolerant of slovenly work in the classroom, and pretentiousness and conceit were effectively punctured by the swift flash of his rapier. Sensitive students sometimes winced under his sarcastic tongue, but the knowledge that he had unwittingly wounded a man of humble heart always brought from him words of gracious kindness that went far to heal the sore. It is well to remember that he was a lifelong sufferer; it was an operation, successful beyond expectation, in 1898 which gave his Church many more years of his service. He never forgot his old students. 'His hand on one's shoulder, twenty years after, and a word of kindly remembrance, would make one's heart glow with pride.'[2] On Easter Sunday morning 1935, he asked leave to pronounce the Benediction at the service in the Friar's Stile Road Chapel, and his voice rang resonant. The worshippers had heard him for the last time.

Less than a week before he died, he spoke to Professor Clogg of what Richmond had been and of what, as he prayed, it always would be, until the tears came into his eyes, and his voice broke. No place on earth was dearer to him than Richmond.

J. Agar Beet became Theological Tutor (1885-1905) after the long service of George Osborn. His name came to the fore with his Commentary on *Romans* ('my *Romans*'), which was followed by other Pauline commentaries. For twenty years he charmed and delighted his students by his rare clarity of mind, his vigorous teaching, his utter contempt for

[1] Quoted by Howard, *Mystics and Poets*.
[2] R. S. Armsby, *ibid.*

all that was obscure and unfair, by the painstaking manner in which he explained and illustrated.

Older readers will remember the controversy which gathered around his name in 1902, when Conference debated his reappointment to his Chair. Many sought to replace him: there was a suggestion that George Findlay be invited to take the position, but he refused to supplant a lifelong friend. A second volume on Immortality was considered to break an engagement entered into after the appearance of the first. But the findings of the Conference Committee did credit to its members when, after declaring that Beet's teaching[1] fell short of our doctrines and contravened them, they continued: 'In regard to the whole case, the Committee recommends, in view of the dread solemnity and mystery of the subject, and the necessity of allowing some freedom of opinion upon it, and out of regard to the fidelity of Dr. Beet to our general system of doctrine, that the Conference take no further action in the matter on condition that Dr. Beet will not teach in our pulpits the doctrine of the book.' Upon acceptance of these conditions, he was reappointed.

Whatever were the views of the fathers of the Church, the storm had little effect on College life, beyond a cheerful cartoon in *Flashlight*. His students remember him with gratitude. R. R. Tregunna has sent us the postcard which Beet sent to him, as to all men called out to circuit, before the first Sunday in his new pulpit, in which he sends kindly and encouraging greetings; and James Lewis has written[2] of 'A Great Fast Day with Joseph Agar Beet'. He also recalls how Beet would dictate full-stops, indented lines, and underlinings. He was always ready to give extra tuition in any subject to help a man. Every lecture with him was an act of worship, and his students never forget the simple piety and beautiful phrasing of his opening words of prayer. He saw the invisible and, seeing, spoke.

J. G. Tasker was appointed Classical Tutor, 1887-91, to deal also with mathematics. He had served four years as

---

[1] It embodied a form of conditional immortality.
[2] *Methodist Magazine*, 1924, p. 593.

Assistant Tutor from 1876, and another term from 1884. In 1891, he went to his even greater work at Handsworth.[1] His life was almost entirely within the College, but from his term in Cannstatt[2] (1880) he acquired a lifelong interest in German theology, and made valuable friendships with German thinkers. Few men sooner got to the heart of a difficult and abstruse book, and in fewer sentences could reveal it to those to whom otherwise it would have remained a sealed volume.

A Handsworth student[3] has written: 'It is hard to define the Doctor's gift to Handsworth'—it was not merely the studies, but his poetry, the heart at leisure from itself, the accessibility of the man. He always had a remarkably detailed knowledge of his students. 'We were dull scholars and slow,' says another student,[4] 'but we came to know our teacher, and to hold him in ever-growing reverence and esteem. He had all the scholar's hatred of superficial and ill-digested knowledge. He knew our limitations—a knowledge that comes hardly to us all! Yet he never let us feel that we were dragging. Perhaps no keener observer ever taught a class. He noted every movement; he could read the degree of our attention. The lessons were great, the teacher was immeasurably greater. He taught much: he inspired more, and always he brought us into the very presence of the great Teacher Himself.'

George Fletcher was House Governor from 1891 to 1909. Himself a Richmond man, he served at Didsbury as Assistant Tutor, and then was Governor at Woodhouse Grove. As Governor of Richmond he won the respect and affection of the men, treating them with frankness and confidence, and even when they were far away on the field his letters and encouragements followed them never-failingly. A shy, reserved man who did not find it easy to unbend, and digni-

---

[1] He gained the unique tribute in 1891 of a petition for his retention, by the Richmond students.

[2] Methodist work in Germany was later handed over to American Methodists.

[3] Mr. Bevan Shepherd, *Methodist Magazine*, 1917.

[4] *Methodist Magazine*, 1912, p. 190.

fied, he showed great kindness and sympathy where there was need; he trusted men, and got the best out of them. His great contribution to the life of Richmond was to be found in his lectures on Pastoral Work and the Polity of the Church, and by his conduct of the class meetings and the sermon classes. His sacramental addresses were an exceptional source of inspiration. To each freshman, says Wilfrid Hannam, he gave a signed copy of Brother Lawrence's *Practice of the Presence of God*. If ever a man walked before God, it was George Fletcher.

We are indebted to C. J. Wright for the following account of *A. S. Geden*, Classical Tutor, 1891–1915: 'Dr. Geden was primarily a scholar, but a scholar with a great yearning to teach. It would be idle to say that he was able to teach every one who sat at his feet. Nature had not endowed him with the electric personality which can arouse the sluggish minds of the mentally apathetic into an unwonted activity. Some of his disabilities (as I know from his cousin, the nonagenarian Dr. Wilkinson of Didsbury) were caused by an attack of typhoid fever when he was a child. The light shone from his mind, not in brilliant, lightning flashes, but in a slow and sometimes seemingly listless stream. His wavering voice, occasionally—as in the beautiful prayers with which his essentially spiritual soul expressed itself at the opening of each day's lectures—breaking into a shrill and cracked note of inward passion, was an index of his spirit. How much he knew! How deeply he felt! And with what difficulty he translated both his knowledge and feeling to others!

'An essential humility lay at the heart of his scholarship. Often I look at the portrait of his father here at Didsbury, where "Alfred", as he was known to his relatives, was born and brought up. The father's face is that of a Christian scholar and saint. It is strangely like that of the Dr. Geden I knew at Richmond. And I am glad to remember that my own Old Testament and Comparative Religion Tutor at our southern College was Assistant Tutor at Didsbury for a year (1883–4),[1] his father having died there in 1882.

'Humility is perhaps the most misunderstood virtue of the

[1] Thus reversing his father's career.—ED.

Christian. The humility of Dr. Geden was of no spurious variety. And what industry he incarnated! When late at night I looked down from my bedroom across the lawn to his house, the light from his study seemed as inevitable as the night itself; and through the uncurtained windows I imagined I discerned him, or his shadow, perhaps standing at his desk as he compared Hebrew texts for his new British and Foreign Bible Society edition of the Old Testament, or—as was sometimes suggested—kneeling before them for a change of physical position. His lectures on the Comparative Study of Religion were, I believe, the most scientific and scholarly then given in a Methodist college. *The Concordance to the Greek Testament* (1897), which appeared over the names of W. F. Moulton and A. S. Geden, is largely the work of the latter.[1] The former's generous acknowledgement of this in the Preface is familiar to students, as also his commendation.

'And how sensitive he was! Few, perhaps, discerned this. One morning some students had, as I imagine thoughtlessly, though after careful planning, arranged that a series of discordant noises should break out in the middle of the lectures. When the bells in the chimney began to clang, and the alarm bells to tinkle from the muffling interior of the desks—shall I ever forget his look? First, of dazed wonderment, then—as realization flooded upon his mind—of a deep pain seen in his white and drawn face, and finally of a flushed anger which none had ever before witnessed. Nor do I think that his primary feeling was from the wound to self, but rather from the disrespect to the beloved Hebrew he was trying to teach the unappreciative.

'Geden's abiding interest in the work of the National Children's Home and Orphanage was an index to a spirit which had drunk deeply of the teaching of Him who said: "Of such is the Kingdom of Heaven." '

From 1904 to 1910 *J. A. Vanes* held the office of Tutor in New Testament Language and Literature, and Philosophy; but all his English work seems little more than an interlude

---

[1] We have not attempted to enumerate the many books, published lectures, or contributions to commentaries, etc., by Richmond's Tutors. See suggestion on p. 144.

in a life whose first love was India. He went there first in 1876, remaining with distinction until 1894, but at the age of sixty-three he went back again in 1916 for another ten years' service. The obituary notice describes him as a man of high intellectual gifts, with an accurate knowledge of Indian languages, and speaks of the personal charm, shrewd wit, and humble, unselfish spirit which greatly endeared him to his brethren. Certainly his great record of missionary service must have borne its witness in the missionary College.

There is a convention that the living should be treated with more reserve than those whose course is run. *Thomas H. Barratt* (Governor 1909–15), who belongs to Didsbury in even greater measure, is happily with us, and speaks for himself in this volume.

Of him, and of *Harry Bisseker* (New Testament and Philosophy, 1910–15) we have this word from L. W. Dickens (1912–14):

'Many of Mr. Barratt's sayings remain with us as jewels of real and memorable wisdom. But it was the man who made such a mark on us—Richmond men will not forget the triumphant faith of a man who passed through deep waters and was so much "more than conqueror" that he brought to us a sense of things unseen and eternal. We shall remember those Communion services, so formally correct and complete, yet bringing the infinite Grace near and real. Some of us scarcely ever repeat parts of that service without hearing his accent. We shall remember his home, the grace and joy of it—no small gift to men soon to have homes of their own. We shall remember his ministries of understanding and sympathy in times of difficulty or sickness. We shall remember his unique discipline. We needed it. Here was no Jovian wrath, no arrogance or prying distrust or sarcasm such as College legends often spoke of, but simple appeal to whatever was decent in us, a trust rarely abused.

'Lesser things are fresh in memory—personal contacts in walk and talk, where men discovered a love of Nature, a warming cheerfulness of spirit, courtesy and a whimsical humour, and much more that made it easier to believe in God, and that God is love.

'Men of that period count his Governorship as an outstanding privilege of their College days, and thank God on every remembrance.

'Mr. Bisseker was a Teacher in the best sense of the word. His tall, donnish figure, with flying gown and gathered books, certainly looked the part, and closer acquaintance found one who was learned without pedantry, who could encourage and appreciate our feeble beginnings, and awaken eagerness such as might bear fruit down the years. We honoured him for his integrity; we loved him for his genial kindness and brotherliness; looking back, we can appraise the thoroughness, accuracy, and the foundation character of the work we did in his classroom. It was amongst the elements that we worked. There were no frills nor fancy theories, nor alluring speculations such as can easily make the New Testament interesting for those who may yet remain comparatively ignorant of it. It might be imagined we failed to see the wood for the trees. By no means. We learned to know the trees; and the exploring of the wood has been for many men a much more intelligent and fascinating pursuit ever since. Not only has the Greek Testament become a different book for us, but I wonder how many men seek for the meaning of things, prepare their sermons, fulfil their pastoral duties and even dig their gardens more thoroughly because of those years of initiation! Belated wisdom and the discipline of inadequacy have confirmed the great and personal debt we owe to Mr. Bisseker, with many another debt which space forbids us to mention.'

★ ★ ★ ★ ★

The Staff which entered the college in 1920 was in control when I entered in 1927. Many times during the research necessary for this section, reading of bygone Tutors—their scholarship, humanity, helpfulness, the watchful care undreamed of by all save the man who has profited by it—I have thought: 'How easily all this could be written about the Tutors I knew!' *W. T. A. Barber* (1920–29), Principal and Resident Tutor, Pastoral Theology and—for one year—

Comparative Religion, lives on in the grateful memory of those who studied under him. Unhappily he cannot assist us in the compilation of this record, although no man living has known more about Richmond. A generation is rising which needs to be instructed in his marvellous career. Born in one mission field, brought up in another; the first Kingswood boy to take the highest position in the Oxford Local and Senior Examinations, a local preacher while still at Kingswood, as successful in all sports as in all studies; taking high honours as a Wrangler at Cambridge, and mixing with his studies a tremendous amount of preaching and open-air work, Assistant Tutor at Richmond, Principal of a high school in Wuchang, colleague in China of the great David Hill, until Mrs. Barber's failing health compelled the return to England, Missionary Secretary, a long successful period at the Leys, and finally Richmond—what a record! When in 1924 he was specially invited to China by the Central China University (a tribute to his work years before), his place was taken by *A. E. Sharpley* for a year.

Though we smiled at his methods during his Church History lectures, and those on Pastoral Theology, and though we loved his frequent appearances in the doorway of the wrong classroom with the query, 'Are you mine?'[1] we admired and respected him. It was the Richmond local newspaper which remarked on one occasion that a very kindly exterior masked (as the reporter put it!) a first-class brain. The table in the long corridor never looked quite the same after his departure, bereft of the curiously folded little notes (perhaps a covey of a dozen at a time) bearing a name outside, and within, the words: 'See me: WTAB'! When Dr. Barber retired, the Committee paid tribute, not only to the obvious things—his learning and so forth—but mentioned his active interest in the public life of Richmond, an interest which, they declared, had improved the local standing of the College.

Of the other Tutors it is happily not necessary to write in so valedictory a fashion. Although *C. Ryder Smith* (1920–40)

[1] As there were not enough classrooms in his time to go round, he used first one and then another.

has retired, he is far from inactive, and at this present is lecturing on the Bible in his own unrivalled way, notably to day-school teachers. From the outset, he exercised a spell upon me which, I am happy to say, remains to this day, and will endure. Richmond men are inclined to feel that those who have not studied the Old Testament under Dr. Smith have not really penetrated to the inner things at all! He undoubtedly is the reason why the Old Testament seems noticeably to mean more to Richmond men than to some others in our ministry. Of course, we all began by trying vainly to imitate that remarkable voice of his (what a splendid instrument it is for the expression of the emotions too deep for words, as we heard it at the Synod at Muswell Hill last year). Richmond men everywhere have celebrated his 'Look it up!' or 'What have you done for me to-day, Mr. ——?' One soon noted that his exact knowledge of the Bible and of theology was reinforced by a similar knowledge of subjects which come more directly under the review of his colleagues—a fact which made for a fine completeness of study. The College Committee have spoken of his special sympathy with the Methodist spirit and tradition, of his assured position in the realm of Biblical scholarship. Students during the earlier part of his time at Richmond recall with what magnificent spirit he withstood the assaults of a very painful muscular complaint, from which he made a fine recovery.

Maldwyn Hughes spoke once of his strength of character and deep convictions: 'He is a good man with whom to go tiger-hunting!' (Any Richmond man would pity the tiger!) 'If I did not know how good he is in the classroom, I should have said that he is at his best in committee. He is calm, clear in head and speech, courteous, never rattled, and tenacious of his point.'

It is vain for me to try to compare the influence of the several tutors of my time. Perhaps the happiest of all the happy memories of *E. S. Waterhouse* (Philosophy, 1920–) are those of useful and pleasant Saturday mornings spent by small groups of men reading for university examinations in his study, with the beautiful panorama of the College uprising across the green lawns, where he, puffing at his pipe, opened up to us entirely new lights upon philosophy. (All the Tutors invariably showed themselves prepared to go the second mile in this way.) How many times have I perused some new work on philosophy or psychology, eagerly made notes to incorporate in my college files, with a feeling that here was something really new—only to find in a later reading of Dr. Waterhouse's notes that a sufficient reference to this 'new' thing (if necessary, a rebuttal) was already duly included in a pithy sentence or so in these notes! As a lecturer he is popular, taking great pains to be interesting and to be clear. He is a Richmond man through and through, and it is good to see the former student (and popular student, at that, to judge by frequent references in the *Flashlight*)[1] seated in the Principal's chair. His own career as a scholar has been distinguished, and in 1928 he was elected to represent the teachers of the Divinity Faculty upon the Senate, subsequently being elected Deputy Vice-Chancellor for the year 1936–7.

He is known to Methodists everywhere to-day for his keen social interests—in temperance, for instance—and for his determination that the Forward Movement *shall* move; and this interest was exemplified at every possible point in the notes which he dictated to us. He was always pleased when a former student wrote for permission to make addresses on social problems from the notes of Richmond lectures. And many (including the writer) have certainly done so without the formality of such permission—though with due acknowledgement!

Some of the most exquisite moments of my college course were spent in the Lycett Room under *F. B. Clogg* (New Testament and Classics, 1920–). Greek is not everybody's fancy, but it is mine. He was always meticulous in the care with which he took us through set books for university examinations—not a particle without its due interest and explanation. And though I still remember the 'grudge' I bore him that morning when he himself translated the final, wonderful chapter on Socrates' death, when *I* wanted to

[1] P. 154.

'Go on' at that point, I am sure that I should always do the same myself! The thoroughness of his New Testament criticism and exegesis, in which his authority has grown steadily within recent years, was remarkable, and his care for the devotional and spiritual realities therein a great challenge. It was sometimes difficult to discern his own views in the care with which he summarized those of others, though sometimes they peeped out, as when, having given a masterly summary on various 'symbolical' treatments of the phrase, 'She left her waterpot', in the story of the Samaritan woman (John iv. 28), he ended his note with the comment (and any Richmond man can imagine the quiet and careful tone): 'It is possible, of course, that the words mean that she left her waterpot!' Reference is made elsewhere to his prowess at games—it was always a delight to see him at tennis, and he frequently played in the college team.

With Dr. Barber's passing from the scene, *Leslie F. Church* (Resident Tutor, Pastoral Theology and Church History, 1929–35) came among us. When we reassembled after his first term, he said to us: 'I thought Richmond was a place—but I find that it is *people*!' Never has a Governor anywhere been more greatly beloved. We were as attracted by his brotherliness and humility as we were appalled by the long hours he worked. I remember that the Chairman and I took it upon ourselves to suggest to him that one's bed *was* better sought before 2 a.m.! His preaching—but all Methodism knows that. His methods with Church history were somewhat different from Dr. Barber's, and his vivid sense of the historic made old and forgotten scenes live again. His talks on English Literature, too, were much valued, as the leadings of a sure guide.

Mention should be made too of the work of two 'visiting Tutors', *C. R. North*, who came in from Egham to take Hebrew between 1923 and 1925, before going to Handsworth, and *W. G. Findlay*, who from 1928 to 1939 came twice weekly from nearby circuits for Classics. He has all the Findlay genius for these things, and no more need be said—except that it is not likely that I should possess anything in the nature of a degree but for his unsparing kindness and patient help. And such a word is spoken because others could say the same. His delight in his subject, and in every interesting by-path into which it may lead, is so obvious. He shows no great or immediate concern with parsings and suchlike; you should know these things before you come. But standing, looking into space with abstracted eyes as he speaks, he sends men to their studies with a new interest and delight.

When Dr. Smith retired, his place as Theological Tutor was taken by *Harold Roberts* (1940–) and in the one year he had with the men before the College was closed, he gained their affection and respect. It is difficult, says a former student, to praise too highly the clarity of his thought and speech, and the high quality and helpfulness of his lectures. One can appreciate that it was not easy to take up a course of lectures where Dr. Smith had laid it down, but it says much for Dr. Roberts that, although his lectures were of a very different kind from those of Dr. Smith, he yet maintained that former high standard. Together with this, his valuable co-operation with the Crusade preparations will be remembered, and there are many men who are indebted to him for his help and advice in personal problems.

S. G. Dimond became Resident Tutor after Dr. Church (1935–41) and, like him, assumed responsibility for College life outside academic bounds, together with lectures on Church History, Pastoral Theology, Methodist Polity, and English Literature—a fairly full sphere! He has concerned himself greatly since he came to Richmond with the state of Richmond's 'treasures'—the paintings and other interesting and valuable things to be found there, as Dr. Ryder Smith had before him. All the men have been grateful to him for his sincere faith, his genuine friendship, his deep concern for their well-being, his humility, tact and wisdom, and will wish him well in his new office of Secretary for Ministerial Training, to which he was appointed last year.

It has seemed better to render thanks in a single word for all that the wives of Richmond's tutors have meant to the men, in representing and supplying many charming things which would otherwise be lost in the stress of monastic life, than to speak especially of those whom I had the good fortune to know. All that could be said of the Tutors' wives in recent years must be equally true of their predecessors. And Richmond gives thanks.

There are Richmond men who have more personal reasons for such thanksgiving—since Tutors have often had families! Two of Osborn's daughters married into the ministry, as did two of Geden's nieces; W. H. Findlay's wife was Alice Hellier; a daughter of Daniel Sanderson became Mrs. J. G. Tasker, and has kindly helped in this record, and another married David A. Rees. Thomas Stephenson married a daughter of George Fletcher. All the world knows of Katherine Barrett and Hugh Price Hughes; and those of us who were there in Dr. Church's day were not without our anticipations of that which has been fulfilled!

In addition to the regular staff of Tutors, Richmond owes much to a long list of talented young men who have held the office of Assistant Tutor. (Their names will be found at p. 160.) The office is never easy to hold, for the position requires dignity and ability, yet accessibility and friendliness. Most of the men have succeeded triumphantly. Some of them returned later as Tutors, at Richmond or elsewhere— W. F. Moulton, J. G. Tasker, W. T. A. Barber, R. Idwal Hopwood, F. B. Clogg; the list also includes the names of W. H. Findlay, W. F. Lofthouse, and Conrad Skinner. W. H. Dyson is remembered on p. 96. Among others, none has left a brighter name than F. W. Kellett. One student recalls him 'pacing the corridor with gait somewhat unequal, and spectacled eyes searching the stone-slabbed floor' or 'in sweater and shorts on the football field' (men said he could kick a ball anywhere he chose). 'I can see him in the College Chapel pulpit, nervous to the point almost of disablement. But I remember the text, "Apart from Me ye can do nothing", and the echoes of that discourse have never been silenced. Kellett was truly a scholar and a saint. He tried his utmost to make us both.' R. J. Wardell, who became well known as a teacher and writer on homiletics, used to tell how Kellett received him in his own study at 6.30 a.m. for special tuition in Greek and Latin. When he reached India, he attained a position of extraordinary popularity among the Brahmin students, and when he died during a furlough in 1904 they had a funeral service for him in India. He was a great scholar, gaining a triple first at Cambridge. 'Jesus, I have tried' were his last words.

Occasionally, too, one or other of the senior students has been appointed 'sub-tutor', to guide freshmen in some simpler subject. David Hill held this post, and G. Kellett Grice, who held it in 1909, took a weekly class in mathematics. He draws a pleasing picture of truants from this class being carried into the lecture-room bodily by their colleagues!

Dr. Smith adds: 'The century falls practically into four equal parts. In the first, Jackson, I think, was the man who dominated the place. In the second, Osborn certainly did. Both he and Jackson were massive men. In the third, Davison's is the leading name, but no one quite dominated.' (Dr. Smith suggested in conversation that Hugh Price Hughes was 'the biggest Richmond man' of this period.) 'Davison and Geden could not see eye to eye, and during Davison's absence Beet went his own inimitable way. In the fourth period, the Staff practised a brotherly equality which had, I think, hardly been reached before.'

STUDIES—AND STUDENTS

E. S. WATERHOUSE, *Student* 1898–1901; *Professor in Philosophy*, 1920; *Principal*, 1940

SOME of us who have been teaching for many a long year end with the opinion that it matters far more how you teach than what you teach! A glance at the story of a hundred years of teaching at Richmond might prove a confirmation of that opinion. In 1845 good Thomas Jackson assured the Committee that the men had instruction in the things which become sound doctrine. He declared that 'Various doctrines have been somewhat copiously expounded . . . referring at the same time to the various forms of error by which the Church of Christ has been annoyed in different ages and countries, and the principal advocates that God has raised up to defend His truth and cause. . . .' We learn too that 'an attempt has been made also to . . . establish the minds of the students in their attachment to Wesleyan Methodism and to supply an antidote to the dogmas of Popery, and to the unwarrantable assumptions of the intolerant men who in the present day so loudly cry, "The Temple of the Lord, the Temple of the Lord are WE!" ' One is left to judge who were the intolerant brethren.

Apparently at first teaching was somewhat indiscriminate, but it soon became clear that educational differences between the men made it needful to divide them into classes, six of which were arranged by John Farrar in 1845. The highest class 'have read in Hebrew the entire Book of Psalms'. But prepare to be astounded yet more, for these supermen also did 'Greek New Testament', together with 'Euripides, Herodotus, with translation into Greek' and in Latin 'all Terence's plays except one'! If after that there is any spirit left in you, prepare to learn that the lowest class took English grammar, geography, history, arithmetic, etc., 'and have been labouring' (apt word, indeed!) 'at the grammars of the Latin and Greek languages', and read in Virgil and the Greek New Testament.

Languages were by no means all that this amazing curriculum held. Moral Philosophy, with weekly tests upon Butler's *Analogy*, and syllogistic practice, together with study of the principal philosophical writers, was the lot of the senior men. Others did 'Natural Philosophy', accompanied by experiments on mechanics, hydrostatics, and hydraulics, pneumatics, acoustics, and heat. It is a fascinating speculation to guess what these 'experiments' might have been. In my days we certainly had many experiments in heat when we tried to light our fires, with certain hydrostatic effects in college 'rags', but these were surely men of sterner mould, for we learn that 'the students have succeeded in a degree far beyond what might have been anticipated'.

Seriously, of course, no educationist can believe that this grandiloquent report of studies represented anything but a veneer of knowledge. It suggests that the Staff tried to do everything; yes, even 'optics' and 'manual astronomy', and the inevitable result surely followed, for as the years go by the curriculum becomes less and less ambitious, even though from 1846 down to 1920 attempts were made to teach all men Hebrew.

The perennial questions of College life were not long in appearing. As early as 1845 the examiners recommended the raising of the educational standard for candidates, to save the Tutors' time in grounding them in elementary studies. Another trouble centre has always been elocution. In testing candidates, the Methodist Church has always been much more concerned with the matter of their sermons than the powers of delivery. No amount of elocution at college will make a bad speaking voice good. Minutes of the College Committee indicate that in 1861 consideration of the matter was urged, and next year professional instruction was advised, only to be rejected in the following year. Upon a layman, Mr. Holden of Oakworth, offering £100 for elocution lessons, however, a year later twelve men were allowed instruction from a Mr. Bell (1864). The suspicious Committee insisted that a Tutor must be present at the lessons, and Mr. Bell objected. This ended the experiment, but it was subsequently resumed under Mr. Charles Plumtree, and in time became a recognized part of the curriculum. Many Richmond students remember the ethereal figure of Professor Richardson, affectionately nicknamed 'Spoof', and his dramatic oratory, whilst in modern days Mr. Field Hyde has laboured strenuously with the varied accents and intonations of the men, and an elocution prize has been given. Another perennial problem, that of the 'fourth year', raised its head in 1874, but not till recent times has a fourth year been a common feature of a college career. A suggestion that elementary music be taught was declined in 1905, owing to 'lack of time'.

Meanwhile, greater matters were astir. In 1892 a conference of teachers from London Free Church colleges urged the establishment of a Theological Faculty and Degree at London University. In 1900, the University, hitherto an examining body only, became by Act of Parliament a teaching University, destined to grow until now, apart altogether from its 'external' side, it is the largest teaching University in the Empire, with more students than Oxford and Cambridge combined. In 1902 the first B.D. examination was held. Richmond obtained a place in the reconstituted University as a divinity school, but the connection was not utilized, though Davison and Geden were members of the Board of Studies in Theology and of the Faculty. None the less, such Richmond men as took the B.D. degree sat as external students till 1915, when the war closed down the College.

Soon after the re-opening in 1920, a University inspection of the College was held. The inspectors reported kindly, but pointed out that the privilege of being a school of the University had been little appreciated, and warned the Staff that it would not be continued if amendment in this respect was not made. The new Staff took the warning seriously, and in a very short time things were mended. A. B. Brockway and a South African student, E. Lynn Cragg, were the first Richmond men to gain the B.D. degree as internal students. That was in 1924, and since then a steady stream of graduates has followed. The Academic Diploma in Theology was established in 1923 with a view to meeting the needs of men who have not matriculated before entry to college, and others whose matriculation did not include Latin or Greek. It is based on the B.D. course, so that, up to a point, men working for degree and for diploma can be taught together, and it has proved of immense value in giving a University test to others than graduates. By this means practically every man in college is enabled to rank as an internal student of London University, and this has strengthened the position of the College in the University itself, in the Union, and in University athletics. None of our colleges has so close a connection with a university as has Richmond. By virtue of the Act of 1926, it became possible for the University to appoint Professors and Readers in Theology, as in other faculties. As the appointment of our Staff is, of course, a matter for Conference, some difficulties arose, which were happily overcome by an arrangement which allowed the Conference to submit the names, and the University freely to grant or withhold recognition of them from their standpoint. Dr. Ryder Smith and Dr. Waterhouse became Professors in 1931 of Theology and of the Philosophy of Religion respectively, and Mr. Clogg Reader in New Testament Studies. In 1937 he also received recognition as Professor.

After the stupendous list of subjects attempted a century ago, our curriculum to-day seems modest. In 1920, when the College reopened after the war, it was shaped by a plan whereby each college should have, in addition to a common block of studies, a subject for special emphasis. At Richmond this was Philosophy, a term which includes logic, ethics, the philosophy of religion, including the non-Christian religions, and a good deal of psychology. For the rest, the curriculum is based on the University requirements in theology. Only men taking the B.D. now study Hebrew, but every man, with insignificant exceptions, studies New Testament Greek. Theology and Church history are of course prominent, and Methodist doctrine and practice naturally find a place. Every man does practical work in connection with the 'Bands'.[1] In old days, when Richmond was a purely missionary college, men learned simple carpentry and medicine. The need for this has vanished, but men still go to the School of Oriental Studies for phonetics, and the missionary centres for short courses relating to overseas work. No doubt as years go by students and studies will vary yet more, but it will always remain that what men are taught is a minor matter. What matters is that their studies shall teach them to think for themselves, to continue to be students for the whole of their lives, and discipline them in that meekness of wisdom which is the hall-mark of the true scholar and of the true Christian.

[1] See p. 155.

V. THE MEN

THE MEN OF RICHMOND

E. J. IVES, 1893–6, WILFRID L. HANNAM, 1901–04, *and* FRANK CUMBERS, 1927–31

WHO are the men of Richmond? There lies before us as we write an old volume, lettered 'Wesleyan Theological Institution: Hoxton and Richmond'. (It might be a fitting part of the Centenary celebration to provide it with a new binding!) We find that the names begin in 1834. John Morris from Salford heads the list, which refers, at that date, of course, to Hoxton. Since Hoxton cannot speak for herself, let Richmond record the names of *John Hunt*, who went to 'Feegee', of *James Calvert* (only it is 'Fegee' this time), of *Luke Wiseman*, who entered in 1839, of *W. B. Pope*. At the close of 1841 we are referred to a later page far on in the book, where we read: 'I know not why this record has been discontinued; in being appointed to the office of Governor, Augt 1858 [*sic*] I have commenced it again.' The words are signed, 'D. Sanderson'. We are greatly indebted to him, and to his sense that Richmond would want to look back as well as forward.

So we turn the pages, and ever and again we thrill to some well-known name—'*He's* one of us!'—in the fellowship that is for ever Richmond. Here in 1844 are three names—*John Dury Geden*, the father of Richmond's A. S. Geden, to become celebrated as Didsbury's Theological Tutor, and a member of the Old Testament Revision Committee; *Benjamin Hellier* is celebrated elsewhere. We encounter, too, the name of *William Morley Punshon*. Not that Richmond can claim to have done much for Methodism's orator, for he went out after only four months. Still, he *was* 'one of us', and we read Joseph Dawson's word with pride: 'Like the gleam of a brilliant, swift-winged flame that flits through a forest, disclosing romantic vistas and unsuspected nooks, was the first passing of Morley Punshon across the rather prosaic tracts of Methodist circuit life.' Yet that active, poetic fire and surpassing oratorical might were joined to a rare serviceable and multiform practical ability; and by his constant journeys through the land he exercised a kind of unofficial and unconscious visitorial influence upon all Methodism.

Charles Garrett and *Joseph Posnett* entered in 1847. Garrett's interest in temperance was equalled by an all-consuming zeal for home missions; he was a pioneer of the Central Hall movement, notably of the work in Liverpool, with the foundation of the Methodist Fire Insurance Company and the *Methodist Recorder* as additional interests! Posnett's name will be for ever linked with Leicester Methodism, which he remade by his constructive and evangelical ability. *Robert Newton Young*, who achieved the rare feat of following his father to the Presidential chair as well as holding the office of Secretary and becoming Assistant Tutor at Richmond and Tutor at Headingley and Handsworth, came in 1850. The 'years' were very small about this time, only two men entering in 1853. It is difficult to-day to discern why, though Rev. T. Naylor advances the suggestion that few men were received because of the great secession in 1849. *David J. Waller* came to Richmond in 1856, notable for his thirty years in the Education Department and his seven as Conference Secretary; 1858 brings five notable names. *Wesley Brunyate*, to become Chairman of the Scotland District and then Governor of Kingswood; *George Fletcher*, destined to govern Richmond (1891–1909); *H. G. Highfield*, famed as an Indian missionary, and *T. Bowman Stephenson* and *W. L. Watkinson*. Brunyate was the first young man to receive a special appointment to East End work; he greatly regretted the brevity of his Richmond term, we are told, and made up for it by voracious and hard reading in circuit.

Bowman Stephenson was to found the Children's Homes and the Deaconess Institute. On the evening prior to his examination for the ministry, he led others gathered at the
I

Westminster Training College in an impromptu open-air meeting! Gifted with all the talents—of daring, preaching power, administrative ability and song—he was distinguished in his circuits for unorthodox and effective tactics, which increased his congregations and incensed his sober superintendents in equal proportion. The minister who in Manchester insisted on standing to preach where the children could see him, found his life-work in London. 'I soon saw little children, ragged, shoeless, filthy, their faces pinched with hunger and premature wretchedness, and began to feel that my time had come. Here were my poor little brothers and sisters, sold to hunger and the devil; and I could not be free of their blood if I did not try to save some of them.' We can but refer also to his musical gifts, expended upon a revision of the Hymn-book, his advocacy of lay representation in Conference and the restoration of Wesley's Chapel. As to his speaking, we read a characteristic Methodist tribute to a May Meeting speech which 'astounded even his friends. It was feared at first that it had ruined the meeting, because no one believed that any one would be able to keep up the enthusiasm. They therefore hastened to take up the collection'!

W. L. Watkinson had but six weeks at Richmond, but himself declared that the influence of Benjamin Hellier, Alfred Barrett and W. F. Moulton was out of all proportion to its brevity. Called out to circuit (it happened to be Stratford-on-Avon!), he made a great reputation as writer and speaker. Methodism has never had a preacher of precisely the same quality. An omnivorous reader, he laid all his reading under contribution for the pulpit. His volumes of sermons were hailed with delight everywhere. He took endless pains with illustrations which were unique in their illuminating effect. Few men ever had a greater power of irony and satire, held under admirable control.

Two years later (1860) there entered Methodism's greatest scientific champion—at least among her ministry—*William H. Dallinger*. Working at a time when it seemed that the declared origin of life might be placed by the scientific world on a materialistic basis, he employed his unique gifts in microscopy, coupled with a phenomenal patience and manipulative skill, in the task of tracing the life history of individual micro-organisms. 'Permitted to labour' on this course, his experiments took six years, and his conclusion was that life can only come from life. Darwin followed his experiments with keen interest and accepted their conclusions; Tyndall declared them to be the most sincere, thorough, and successful piece of scientific work he had ever met; Huxley, a close friend, nominated him as Fellow of the Royal Society. At a time when many Christians were anxious over the impact of science upon faith, his voice was potent, reassuring and enlightening. The same year brought *Josiah Hudson*, who did great educational work in Bangalore, gaining a unique position in Mysore State.

One of Richmond's greatest sons entered in 1861—*David Hill*. It is impossible to do him justice here; fortunately Dr. Barber's biography is available. As a student, he conducted a Bible class for the Tutors' children, and Miss J. E. Hellier has spoken of what it meant to them. After a year as Sub-Tutor, he offered for China, opened to the Western world in the year when he entered College. In 1865 he was among the first six missionaries. His health failing, he recuperated in Japan, and returned to spend thirty-two years in China. His whole aim was to be one with the Chinese that he might show them Jesus; he dressed in their manner and lived in hovels; he gave up all things for Christ, including the idea of marriage. He died at the age of fifty-six, eaten up by the zeal of his fight for China, against famine, opium, and disease, against indifference and persecution.

Dr. Barber's book abounds with vivid pictures. We see Hill wrapping young Barber round with his own blanket to shield him from a night's soaking rain as they went up the great river together; we hear the word of the drunken river captain, disparaging all white men, but suddenly sobered and crying, "There's one man whom every one knows and we all believe in. He is a true Christian, if ever there was one!' We see the man who was chosen, by the Chinese who had vilified him, to distribute the poor relief which they would not entrust to any one of themselves. The memorial tablet in

York Centenary sums it up: 'Being moved by the Holy Ghost, he gave his life with his many talents, large opportunities and all his substance[1] for thirty-two years to the evangelization of Central China, with a generosity that knew no stint, with an earnestness that never grew weary.' Such a one called others to his side—there was a time when practically every Methodist missionary had come to Central China at his personal call.

J. Agar Beet (see p. 110) entered in 1862, and we read of *J. Milton Brown* and *Owen Watkins* in 1863. *Milton Brown* had gifts of administration which proved God-given in peculiarly difficult times in Ceylon and Calcutta. He was the real maker of the Bengal District, and later had responsibility for all the North India work. He did much to bring about the present effectiveness of Methodist Army work in India. And at the end of his life his still lively evangelical zeal found expression in the stablishment of the work at East Barnet, near his suburban London home. *Owen Watkins* wanted to be a missionary, and though at first adjudged unfit, he did get to South Africa in 1876. His strenuous service there was a great blessing to rapidly developing causes, and he organized the work in Transvaal, Swaziland, and Mashonaland, winning the confidence of Cecil Rhodes himself. He explored new fields north of the Limpopo with *Isaac Shimmin* —another Richmond man (1883)—a Rhodesian pioneer, the friend of Kruger and Rhodes. With a powerful personality and strong will, he did great work in many special tasks before ill-health brought him home. He then did notable work in English circuits, and was a great administrator. Small in stature, but sturdy, endowed with a trumpet voice, he was a terror to the 'platform' at Conference—his rising often betokened fireworks!

Another devoted missionary entered in 1864—*R. H. Moreton*. Born in Buenos Aires, he worked for forty-six years to bring the dawn of religious freedom in Portugal, and outlived (or outloved) bitter persecution, to earn the gratitude of many.

In our judgement, *Hugh Price Hughes* (1865) and *David*

[1] Which was considerable.

RICHMOND COLLEGE

Hill were the greatest of Richmond's sons. 'It is difficult to write of such a man', says Hughes's obituary notice. 'A fervid preacher, a passionate denouncer of social wrongs, an orator, speaking with a vehemence almost startling; a debater of unsurpassed readiness and skill, and of extraordinary energy and force.' Certainly we sympathize with that writer!

He dominated Richmond with his intense vitality and resourcefulness. He, too, held a Bible class for the tutors' children. Captain of cricket, his enthusiasm for study was equally intense. Elsewhere we treat of his stand against the segregation of missionary students and we note the future vehement temperance reformer standing up for the students' ancient 'right' to beer! Methodism has long treasured the story of Katharine Barrett, the Governor's daughter who came collecting missionary pennies along the study corridors, and who became his partner in mighty works, exercising a gracious influence at Kingsway to this day.

Every writer has been at pains to do him something approaching justice. Arthur Walters calls him 'Richmond's most interesting and remarkable personality'. Another writer enjoys a Cockney woman's word: 'Ain't 'e lovely, dear? Ain't 'e lovely?' His war-cries are remembered: 'Methodists, wake up!' 'Moderate men, my dear sir, have been the curse of manhood!' 'Believe me, even West London will become the City of God!' 'Never', wrote Miss J. E. Hellier, 'had I heard such daring plans, such boundless hopes; never seen such joyous energy. Supremely a man of prayer, with a celerity which took our breath away and brought us on our knees before we quite knew where we were, he would say, "Let us pray!" He literally wept over the sins and sorrows of the poor girls in Piccadilly.' At his death a cry, as of keen personal bereavement, went up from tens of thousands of mourners. He was the Nonconformist conscience incarnate (only positive, not negative; its purifying flame, not a freezing breath).

Hugh Price Hughes was perhaps God's greatest gift to Methodism since Wesley. He embodied the new 'Forward Movement'. Mrs. Hughes has written of his determination to put aside preaching eminence, to make himself of no account, that men should hear not him, but Christ. Conference cheered and clapped his election as President—an unprecedented scene. He was a great fighter—'at his best when there was something to combat, some evil to be denounced'. He was a born leader of men—he had only to unfurl his flag, says George Jackson, and at once men rallied to it. Said George Jacob Holyoake at his death: 'The ethical side of Christianity has hardly dawned, and Mr. Price Hughes was one of its rays.' He died when only fifty-five.

A man of like spirit entered in 1866—*Josiah Mee*, a born home missioner. Associated in the Bolton District with Thomas Champness and the Joyful News Mission, he laboured valiantly, too, in the temperance cause. When he was nearly seventy, in 1913, he opened a new Methodist venture in the South Yorkshire coalfield, and for five years visited, incessantly, preaching in the open-air, selling books in the market-places. Wherever he went, the work of God revived; he was a daring evangelist.

Marshall Hartley came in 1867, showing even then the budding of gifts equally necessary, though diverse. Fellow students remembered the astonishing speed at which he worked (not unnecessary in a young man appointed Assistant Classical Tutor to Dr. Moulton), the perfect order of his study, his genial, brotherly fellowship and hearty singing. He spent thirty-one years at Mission Headquarters, visiting overseas fields and helping missionaries both by his constant advocacy and effective skill. He was a most expert Conference Secretary for seven years, and placed the secretariat of most Connexional causes under obligation for his help. 'The best and quickest minute secretary I have ever known', wrote one committee-man, who went on to praise his expertness in reducing the sense of tangled meetings to explicit resolutions.

We speak of *G. G. Findlay* elsewhere (p. 108)—he came in 1869. Another accomplished scholar was *Henry Haigh* (1873). He seems to have done everything possible during his twenty-seven years in India, beginning with Mysore in 1874. Sent straightway to a place where no one could speak

English, he mastered the Kanarese language, spending five years on the revision of the Bible, and accomplishing great things in the foundation of Christian literature and newspapers. Returning home, he later became Missionary Secretary. He was always planning something that might some day become glorious fact—and he died in Hankow in the midst of a journey which by the rules of human wisdom should never have been undertaken. He had the mind of a statesman, building his policies on deep and sagacious principles.

John G. Tasker (1873) later became a Tutor in his own College before going to Handsworth—also our debtor for W. F. Lofthouse. *Amos Burnet* (1878) gave many years of service in Mysore and Bangalore, and was sent in 1902 to the Transvaal, where for seventeen years he wisely guided our work, overcoming the difficulties which arose after the Boer War. From 1919 he was Secretary of the Missionary Society. *J. W. Lord* (1878) served nineteen years in Honduras and thirteen in Barcelona and Madrid. In 1879 *William H. Findlay* entered, going to Madras a year later. For twenty years he was Principal of the Negapatam High School, then founder of the Mannargudi college which bears his name. Missionary Secretary from 1900, he had an active part in 'Edinburgh, 1910', after which he spent a valuable year in taking the Edinburgh message to the Churches. The last five years of his life he spent in Bangalore, studying and surveying missionary conditions, despite considerable suffering. He died in Madras in 1919.

Another great Indian name is that of *William Goudie.* It stands immediately following Findlay's (they were of the same age, too, almost to a day). After two exceptionally strenuous years at the College, he went to Madras, and royally used his great strength and apparently limitless powers of endurance. He soon became a fluent Tamil speaker, and gained general recognition as a missionary leader and thinker, and as the friend and champion of the outcastes, among whom he nursed cholera victims with untiring tenderness. He made a great reputation at the Edinburgh Missionary Conference (1910), and thereafter was known everywhere as a great missionary statesman. 'I cannot find room for myself at the foot of the Cross', is one of his great words, 'until I have found room there for the whole round world.' His death came in 1921, when he was President-designate of Conference. We remember, too, his brother, *James Goudie*, who entered in 1884.

J. A. Elliott, the great vernacular preacher of Faizabad, came in 1880. The son of a soldier stationed in India, and brought up with great devotion by a widowed mother, he was possessed of an unparalleled knowledge of Indian languages and ways, which made him mighty in Christ's service.

1882 saw the arrival of *A. E. Restarick*, whose field was Ceylon; and the following year two other great workers overseas—*W. W. Holdsworth* and *W. A. Cornaby*. Holdsworth had behind him the tradition of a father who worked his way out to Jamaica, and lived at his own expense, so keen was his desire to preach Christ. The son did great work in Mysore, especially in time of plague, and completed the Missionary Society's *History* when that task fell from G. G. Findlay's hands. Cornaby is remembered for his labours in Central China. He exercised varied gifts—music, painting, science, and many practical arts—in the task of bringing the more cultivated classes of Chinese to Christ, and attained a marvellously intimate knowledge of Chinese modes of thought.

One of the pioneers of our Burmese work, *A. H. Bestall*, came in 1884. His going followed upon the annexation of Upper Burma, and he established schools and a leper home, and also translated hymns and the New Testament into Burmese. In 1920, at great personal sacrifice, he went out again to deal with difficulties resulting from the war, and was awarded the Kaisar-i-Hind gold medal for his services to the Empire. 'He was anointed with the oil of gladness above his fellows', says the obituary notice. 'His radiant spirit seemed unconquerable, and his genius for making friends enabled him to win the souls of men.' The same year saw *J. H. Bateson*, who also went to Burma, as a chaplain, beginning there, and continuing in India, the remarkable work for which he became distinguished. He gained the support and confidence of successive Commanders, like Lord Kitchener, and was able at the same time to make the private feel that he was a friend. Dr. Ryder Smith tells us that he has gone with him into a Bombay canteen, and has seen him draw men from the bar to listen to an informal temperance talk. In 1909 he returned to become Secretary of the Navy and Army Board, and in the First World War did much to alleviate the lot of the ordinary soldier and to maintain Methodism's position with the authorities.

We find *George Jackson* entering in 1885. Declining Hughes's invitation to join him at the West London Mission, he went to Edinburgh to lay the foundations of the Mission in 1888. He quickly gathered a fine congregation in that city of famous preachers, under the very shadow of Alexander Whyte's church, and he preached there for eighteen years, introducing the 'daring innovation' of evening services, before going to Toronto. There, after a successful pastorate,[1] he began the work in college which he continued at Didsbury. Many think that his place is the pulpit and not the tutor's chair, however important the chair may be, for his supreme interest is in the art and practice of preaching. His many books reveal his mind on literary as well as religious subjects, and Methodism knows him best by the 'Parson's Log' in the *Methodist Recorder* and as 'G. J.' of the *Manchester Guardian*.

1886 brought *Edward Nicholson*, destined to live but a few months in the deadly Honduras climate, but witnessing conversions every Sunday during his time at Richmond; *Samuel R. B. Solomon* from Cape Coast, 'a great West African', says James Lewis, 'about six feet six in height, of princely race, with a prince's bearing, and with the gentlest, burring voice imaginable, loved and admired by all'; *T. Morcom Taylor*, known for his labours in our English circuits. It brings, too, the name of *Samuel Parkes Cadman*.

His life and ministry lay outside British Methodism; but Richmond and Methodism alike have never forgotten him. As recently as 1927 the *Old Chariot* contained a valuable article by him which paid tribute to the College and its

[1] See *Methodist Magazine*, 1912, p. 573.

Tutors. 'My loyalty for the place', he says, 'is undivided and indivisible. The three years I spent . . . lifted some veils for me.' He especially revered F. W. Kellett, whose help and guidance were extremely valuable to him. His visits to England were always an inspiration, and till his death he remained a member of the little Shropshire chapel where he began. Dr. Beet once said: 'Without doubt, of all the men who studied under me at Richmond, Samuel Parkes Cadman showed the greatest promise.'

From his beginning in New York, his reputation spread widely and rapidly. At thirty-six he became minister of the Central Congregational Church in Brooklyn. Men have called him the greatest apostle of Peace—he made a supreme contribution to religious tolerance. Jews, and Christians, both Protestant and Roman Catholic, and men of all classes gathered at his funeral, and a Jewish Rabbi declared: 'His heart beat with sympathy and love for all men, regardless of race, colour and creed.' As a famous radio preacher, his words reached the hearts of thirty millions of people, and his words circulated in a hundred newspapers. Dr. H. B. Workman, his lifelong friend, has spoken of his marvellous preaching power, and his unfailing capacity for making human contacts.

Harold C. Morton entered in 1891, and became a Sub-tutor. He is remembered as independent, an orator, courageous in the concerns he held to be true and righteous, but reserved in his relations with the men. Later he was one of the two chief defenders of Fundamentalism. *C. Ensor Walters* came in 1892. He speedily took his place as one of the 'star preachers' of the College, with a voice which became known as 'Walterian'; but the men of his time did not generally discern in him that organizing power which led to his work for Methodism in London. He will long be remembered as Secretary of the London Mission, where he carried on his father's work. He won the good opinion of George Bernard Shaw when he served with him on the St. Pancras Borough Council.

Two great modern missionaries came in the same year—*C. H. Monahan* and *C. W. Posnett*. The life of both has been given to India, Monahan's name being associated with

RICHMOND COLLEGE 139

Madras, and the award of the Kaisar-i-Hind shows the value set upon his work by Government. He remains in the Far East still, and has added to his normal work much labour connected with the South India Church Union Scheme. The same award was made to Posnett, the most famous missionary of our years. His name will be for ever linked with Medak. Gathering round him a fine band of helpers, he was able to establish in Medak an orphanage, a hospital, a theological training college for evangelists, and to build a great church in thirty-eight years. When he went in 1895 the community numbered 4,254; when he left it had risen to 121,098, and in the year 1942 it numbered 129,656, for he was at the heart of one of the great mass movements which have stirred the hearts of all who look for the Kingdom of God. Just as fifty years ago, when he charged down the football field, men were apt to scatter themselves lest a bull of Bashan should treat them as ninepins, so, before his energy and force, difficulties have been brushed aside and his work urged forward by a dominating will and boundless courage—and the grace of God.

1893 brought *Owen Spencer Watkins*, whose career is unique in Methodism, and has carried him into spheres seldom reached by Methodist preachers. He hoped to carry on his father's work, but his health prevented him going to Mashonaland, and he went into Army work at Malta. In 1897 he was in Crete with an expeditionary force; the following year found him with Kitchener in the Sudan, where he was one of the chaplains at the Gordon Memorial Service at Khartoum. Two years later, when war broke out in South Africa, he arrived just in time to be shut up in the Siege of Ladysmith for over three months. In 1914 he was at once sent to France and was in the historic retreat from Mons, he later became Principal Chaplain on the Italian front, where he was in command of chaplains of all denominations. In this capacity he had the experience, unique for a Methodist minister, of diplomatic audience with the Pope. He was then ranking as a brigadier-general. In 1925 he was appointed an Honorary Chaplain to the King, the first Nonconformist to be so appointed. After the war he became

Assistant Chaplain-General, and in 1924 Deputy Chaplain-General, with a room in the War Office. He is the most be-ribboned man in our ranks, and was given the C.M.G. and a C.B.E., as well as an Italian order. Retiring, he became Administrative Padre to Toc H.

J. G. Darrell (1893) became Principal of another Richmond College—at Galle, Ceylon.

Edgar W. Thompson (1893) left the College early to go to some great work in India for twenty-five years, and then became one of the Secretaries at the Mission House. Henry Haigh once said that he had it in him to write the best apologia for Christianity against Hinduism.

Owen J. Letcher (1894) was also a chaplain to the Forces, served in France and won a D.S.O., becoming Assistant Chaplain-General, and succeeding Watkins as Senior Wesleyan Chaplain in France. *A. Trevellick Cape*, of the same year, also served in 1914, and was awarded an M.C., after working in some of the British garrisons. 1895 saw the arrival of two of Methodism's 'business men', although their circuits have thankfully avowed them to be more than that! *Edgar C. Barton*, our Book Steward, through whose hands this book has passed in its preparation, and *William Humphrey*, who served the Chapel Committee in Manchester. We know how essential both posts are in the general smooth working of Methodism. Mention should be made of *Oliver J. Griffin*, of the same year, whose boast it is that for thirty-one years he was able to stay in West Africa, and who is now teaching Nigerian dialects at Oxford for the Government. Nor ought *Charles Phillips Cape* to be forgotten for his fine bit of pioneering work amongst the Doms of Benares. He has often proved his valiancy as a warrior for Christ in championing unpopular causes.

William F. Lofthouse came in the same year direct from the Bermondsey Settlement and Oxford, with social reform in his blood, and scholarship which shaped his career along tutorial paths both at Richmond and Handsworth. He struck awe into some of his contemporaries by writing lecture notes in Greek! *R. Moffat Gautrey*, who went to Mashonaland, should also be named, for after ill-health compelled his

RICHMOND COLLEGE 141

return, he became known as a true evangelist and fearless missioner in this country. *Edgar J. Bradford*—'of Italy'— came in 1896.

The reader will note our observance of a closer rule of reticence as we approach contemporary days, but mention should be made of *Frederick J. Pope* (1897), a man who has served English circuits faithfully and with distinction, of *W. W. Gibson*, of the same year, pioneer missionary of Hunan, followed Chinawards by *J. S. Helps* (1899) and *W. H. Pillow* (1900). *George Sara* (1897) is remembered by his fellows, as the true originator and begetter of a College song, with a chorus which went:

> '*All at sea, up a tree,*
> *Up a tree, all at sea,*
> *With my Ethics, Logic, Psychologee;*
> *I am also very weak*
> *In my Hebrew and my Greek,*
> *And I weary even meek Doctor B.*'[1]

The song has passed, but more recent men know the feeling.

G. Gower Cocks, who came in 1898, went to Royapettah, Madras, after a year. He did a great work among the educated classes in the important student centre of Triplicane. Suddenly smitten down in 1902, he was buried in the presence of such a multitude as no Christian cemetery in India had seen before.

A. J. Revnell entered in 1898, and has from 1901 until this present time, not only lived in India, but for it, with a devotion beyond all praise. The same year brought *E. S. Waterhouse* (see p. 118). *Walter James*, whose great preaching power gave promise of rich fruit, came in 1899, living tragically few years.[2] *P. Middleton Brumwell*, entering in 1900, served first for twelve years in Ceylon, and became a chaplain early in the first World War, rising to be Deputy Chaplain-General, from which office he retired in 1943

[1] Hannam insists that the last line ran, 'And I'm not prepared for thee, Doctor B.'—from which we may draw our own conclusions!
[2] See Carrier's tribute in *The Unveiled Heart*.

—K.H.C., C.B.E., M.C., with two mentions in despatches, 'Brummy' to men everywhere, and Honorary Chaplain to the King.

John E. Reilly, M.C. (1902), left his mark on all his contemporaries. An Irishman by birth, and a Durham pitman by calling, he lived a dissolute, godless life until manhood, and was converted by reading the New Testament in Durham Gaol. Walking with two ministers to preach his trial sermon, he said: 'The last time I came down this road, it was between two policemen.' Coming to Richmond an older man than most, he put his neighbours to shame by his determination to profit by every moment of his stay. 'I have so much lost time to make up for', he used to say. On the Indian mission field he did magnificent work in the Kolar gold fields, and as a chaplain in France. Returning to England, he worked with equal devotion amongst the miners, whose habits and temptations he knew so well. A life of singular beauty and usefulness ended, all too soon by human judgement, in a Manchester street accident in 1929. His biography—alas! now out of print—tells a story that Richmond men do well to treasure.

Another who has rendered distinctive service to his generation is *Jean Scarabin* of St. Brieuc in Brittany. His advent in 1903 created a stir, particularly when it was found that the Welsh students and he were easily able to understand each other. We can only pray that the fine missionary work that Scarabin has done throughout the years has survived the cruel test of war. His son followed him to Richmond in 1931. *Ira G. Goldhawk* (1903), *G. Osborn Gregory* (1905), and *Harold G. Fiddick* (1911) have served great missions in Methodism, the last-named being now head of the world-famous Manchester and Salford Mission. *Thomas Tiplady's* (1906) contribution to modern evangelism calls for recognition; he has been a pioneer in the use of the cinema as a means of proclaiming Christ, and his work in Lambeth for more than twenty years, though rudely interrupted by the war, which destroyed his hall, still goes forward.

Among Richmond's gifts to her sister colleges may be named *Vincent Taylor* (1907). He has made wide contributions to theological learning, and is principal at Headingley, while *C. J. Wright* (1909) went to Didsbury in 1930. In the same year came *A. E. Southon*, who has served West Africa and the Missionary Society, *A. Gordon James*, going to fine service in London, Edinburgh, and Lancashire, and one who, no longer in our ministry, is perhaps our greatest man of letters—*Edward Thompson*. He worked at Bankura, Bengal, from 1910 to 1922, gained a Military Cross in the war, and is known everywhere to-day for his poems, books, and plays. It is not too fanciful to see a foreshadowing of his present style in an article sent home to the *Old Chariot* (No. 4, 1912, p. 43). 1912 saw the entry of *H. Stanley Southall*, another of our great missioners, and *E. Carvan Young*, whose early death deprived Methodism of a choice, quiet soul.

Richmond may well be proud that London's two premier Free Church pulpits are filled by her sons. Although *Leslie D. Weatherhead* (1913) ministers in the famous Congregational City Temple, he abides a Methodist. As a wireless preacher, his fame is in all the Churches. Seven years later *W. Edwin Sangster* came to Richmond (from Handsworth), and now proclaims the gospel from the Central Hall pulpit at Westminster. He has shown himself a scholar as well as a preacher. He is proud of Methodism, with a pride somehow peculiar to those of us who were not born within the camp, and has succeeded latterly in stressing the glories of Wesley Day.

Men of younger Richmond generations are already proving themselves in many fields. The perspective is yet too short to speak of them by name, but there is knowledge of their work—in the lecture-rooms of Caenwood in Jamaica, in the new field of Aruba, in battlegirt Malta, or in Jersey's isolation.

Richmond, closed for two wars, has known other losses in them both. A plate in the Entrance Hall bears the names of C. Rowley Barker, T. Kenneth Barnsley, W. H. Dimmock, Herbert Green, Walter E. Hawkins, and T. Jasper Shovel, all killed in the First World War. The name of W. Hubert Dyson is also there; he had just been appointed Assistant Tutor when the call came overseas (see p. 96). Already the

Second War has taken its toll, and Ernest W. Funnell (1930) was killed in Burma, helping his men, and received mention in despatches for distinguished conduct.[1] Hubert Daniels, E. Howard Metherell, Robert W. Pridmore, and Thomas Russell are in the enemy's hands as prisoners of war. We pray, not only for their safety, but that still they may be empowered to do the work of their high calling wherever they find themselves. Roy L. Pitkin (1936), who joined the R.A.F. as a combatant, is missing.

It has not proved possible, either in this section or that dealing with the Tutors, to give details of the many books which Richmond men have written, or of their contributions to encyclopaedias and famous commentaries. But it has occurred to us that a few shelves in the beautiful new Library could be filled by making a collection of Richmond's own gifts to literature and learning! Such a cross-division might affront the Librarian's scheme, but would be a testimony to what the men have done. They have contributed worthily, too, to the series of Fernley Lectures, and they have four hymns in the present book: Morley Punshon's 'Sweet is the sunlight after rain' (662) and 'We rose to-day with anthems sweet' (666), G. Osborn Gregory's 'Spread the table of the Lord' (757), and Bowman Stephenson's 'Lord, grant us like the watching five' (786).

Richmond men have played their part in other lands—notably South Africa, where a number have reached the Presidential Chair. We have treated of Owen Watkins and Isaac Shimmin (p. 132). Then there was *George Weavind* (1869), the first resident minister in the Transvaal, and *William B. Cawood* (1870) had gone out in 1871, penetrating into the hinterland. *F. J. Briscoe* (1884), scholarly, a fine preacher, microscopical enthusiast, first settled on the Witwatersrand gold field, and generally was a pioneer in the Johannesburg District. *G. H. Eva* (1888), a missionary's son, born in South Africa, did a great evangelizing work among the natives, speaking fluent Bantu. *Edwin Bottrill* (1891), who reached the Transvaal in 1896, has done most distinguished service as Secretary and Chairman of the Trans-

---

[1] *Methodist Recorder*, March 18, 1943, and July 15, 1943.

vaal District, and as President of the South African Conference. He is a skilled administrator, noted for sound judgement and remarkable foresight, trusted and beloved by native ministers and people. *Ernest Titcomb*, forsaking Headingley, entered Richmond in 1894, and came to be acknowledged as South Africa's outstanding preacher. All over Central Africa, as well as in the Union, men listened to his broadcast messages. He was President in 1931. While he was at the Metropolitan Church, Cape Town, his church would be filled with the leading politicians of all parties.

Richmond has played a great part in our evangelizing work in France. What would French Methodism be without *Moïse Alain* (1898) and *Auguste Faure* (1894)? In earlier days the preachers for Ireland were trained in our Colleges, but the College in Belfast (1868) and Edgehill (1919) have carried on that work for years now, and the same applies to France, Australia, and South Africa.

So we take our leave of this old book, having named a man here and there because that name has become famous among the people called Methodists. But we are all the more moved by our journey through its pages because we know that among the hundreds of names within it there is hardly one which does not stand for things precious in God's sight. 'He was a man of wide reading, and this was combined with chaste thinking, great reverence of spirit, and intense earnestness. He manifested the Christian spirit of helpfulness and self-forgetting devotion.' That was written of *J. Harvey Gathercole* (1878), but it might have been written of hundreds of Richmond's other sons.[1] Richmond men have moved widely in this land and every land, serving God, and thanking Him for what they learned of Him at Richmond.

I may be permitted to speak of those with whom I have collaborated in this section. A lifelong friend of *E. J. Ives* (1893) writes of him: 'Quiet, scholarly, widely read, possessed of deep spiritual insight, and a preacher whom the most devout, as well as the most intellectually alert, always find

[1] *Roger Jones, Circuit Minister*, Richard Pyke, Epworth Press, 3d., says what needs to be said about this.

K

stimulating. His literary output has been considerable.' It was George Jackson who once called him 'one of our leading Methodist bookmen'. He was my first superintendent out of College, and I owe him much. *Wilfrid Hannam* (1901) heard my trial sermon at Trinity, Wood Green, and has been a generous friend ever since. He is a man of striking presence, and, like Ives, has served in many of our most important circuits. Now he occupies the Chair of the London Southwest District, with the pundits of Westminster in his charge! —and he holds the position as few men could. He is known as a preacher—and as a man without fear.

MEMBERS ONE OF ANOTHER

Frank Cumbers, 1927–31

In a university, someone has said, men learn most about—men. This is abundantly true of Richmond. Resourceful administrators of Methodist polity, and chairmen who calm the storms of Sunday school councils and choir meetings, learned their first lessons in the conduct of meetings at 'Seats', where second- and third-year men do their best to trap unwary first year 'Monitors' with amendment after amendment, in addition to the one already on hand, 'substantive propositions', and the rest! Tea-clubs, arbitrarily formed, become the closest fellowships earth knows; evermore their members think gratefully of one another. In Benjamin Hellier's 'Life' there is mention of 'Taylor's levee'—daily forgatherings, at which theological papers were read on Monday afternoons, and the arrival of the *Watchman* on Thursday mornings filled the study with conversation. So all things strengthen the bond, whether fellowship in study, prayer, walks, campaigns, or mission bands.

G. G. Findlay once wrote: 'There is nothing quite like the Methodist colleges. They gather young men of almost every rank and previous occupation, of every type of disposition and degree of culture, the Honours graduate perchance side by side with the mechanic, united only in their spiritual experience and Methodist convictions, and their approved call to preach the Gospel. Their schooling has in many cases been early broken off; the fallow years, spent in acquiring a business or handicraft, have made regular study strange and difficult. They have formed habits of independence not easily submitted to the restrictions of college rule, and have learned to exercise powers of usefulness and gifts of speech, winning perhaps a perilous admiration, which may dispose them to regard the drudgery of study as a superfluous affliction.' But he goes on to pay tribute to the marvellous use which these men make of their new opportunities.

An important point may be mentioned here. It is greatly to the credit of Methodism that a man may become a minister whatever his financial position. Men pay what they can, and this policy has been abundantly repaid. Methodism wants the *men*, and gets them. There are even grants for special cases of need, such as may often arise during a three or four years' course. The College Chairman himself may be the poorest man in the place, receiving a grant, for that matter. But the House Governor alone knows these things.

Such a place is a little city in itself. It has proper forms of government—the offices of College Chairman and Secretary are coveted places. Just because of the varied experiences in the former lives of the students, a man can be found for most things that are necessary: the College Treasurer will formerly have been a clerk or accountant; the Plan Secretary must be one apt with records and accurate. 'The Traditions of Richmond' (see p. 148) shows that the College Auditor has thirteen separate systems of accounts to consider. The 'Finance Committee' meets regularly, and the businesslike methods and minutes of the Clears Committee have become a revelation in recent years, even since my own time. There are, roughly, no less than eighty-four offices to which men are elected, besides many committees.

Some of the offices look a little strange—the College Policeman,[1] the 'Bishop of Ellerker' (whose sole annual duty

[1] There is an amusing account of this office by M. H. Russell, *Old Chariot*, No. 1.

was apparently to visit a nearby girls' college at the proper season, to solicit help for the Missionary Garden Party), the 'Hyderabad Correspondent'. There used to be a Boating Secretary, a Photographic Secretary, and a Chess Captain— even a 'Crest China Curator'. It is pleasing to note that the present minister of the Central Hall was once Captain of the Fire Brigade!

There is continuity, yet discontinuity, between one generation and another. Again and again, in reading College magazines and minutes, one sees the same 'bright ideas', the same complaints, the same jokes about the studies. One year it is resolved to buy the railway companies' time-tables, instead of Bradshaw; the next year reverses this decision. At one time the *Daily Telegraph* is dropped from the Reading Room in favour of the *Daily Herald*: at another, the *Daily Mail* is to be substituted for the *Daily Express*, or the *Humorist* is replaced by the *New Statesman*. The cooking, the ineffectiveness of the heating arrangements, and the like seem to have run like a theme-song through the Students' Minutes from the very first!

Richmond's parliament is 'Seats', a meeting for business (serious and otherwise) held after dinner and supper each day, together with statutory business meetings during the year. The Monitors for the week preside at 'Seats', which is the occasion for much cheerful banter as well as business. Each man is Monitor in turn—just as each man used to take a turn in carving the joints (very often to Matron's horror when she surveyed the resultant relic! The present Matron has the meat carved before it comes into Hall—and saves much meat!).

Kenneth Underwood has written of 'The Traditions of Richmond'[1]—a volume compiled at Dr. Dimond's suggestion, which is beside me as I write. Even the College songs are there—looking, I may add, remarkably nonsensical! Are these the words that went with such gusto when old So-and-So and Thingummy bawled them? The compilation is good, and Richmond owes much to Underwood and his colleagues.

[1] Pp. 31, 157.

As he peruses this document, a Richmond man of even a dozen years ago is bound to be struck by the increasingly democratic spirit in College business, yet also by an increasing ceremony. There are more Committees. The College Precentor has a nicely bound 'hymn-book' containing the hymns sung on ceremonial occasions. A gown is now worn by the man who conducts prayers. Subjects are allotted for Morning Prayers (though this has been a feature of the College life often and again in its history). But certain ceremonies have been dispensed with—for instance, rags, though my own unregenerate soul found some pleasure in reading, in the 'Traditions', of one rather uncomfortable welcome reserved for the First Year.[1] In the demure typescript before me, it looks even more uncomfortable than when I felt it myself.

To 'rag' or not to 'rag' was a big issue a dozen years ago. The present Principal, Dr. Waterhouse, strongly disapproved of ragging,[2] and I remember even now the dinner session of 'Seats' at which the custom was formally abolished. Yet much as our ancestors enjoyed their ragging, it must be admitted that there is a great deal to be said for the present method of welcoming the First Year with an introduction ceremony, commenced in 1930, which seeks to portray the spirit and traditions of Richmond. The incoming men sign the 'Book of the Generations' (a beautifully produced volume) and hear the story of the war-cry, together with an account of the College tradition, in its three parts—general, home, and overseas.

One new ceremony certainly sounds practical—the election of the war-cry leader. He is chosen by actual prowess. Candidates stand on the football field, and shout the war-cry towards the rest of the men, assembled at the main door! Again, even the 'new Richmond' unbends, too, to the extent of allowing the baptism of the College Baby. 'The nature of the ceremony is left to the imagination of the Committee appointed' (another committee!).

[1] In fact, some informal ragging advantageously survives.
[2] He praised the institution in an *Old Chariot* article (No. 12, 1921) but it is fair to add that this was ragging of a different kind.

Among all ceremonies, that of Rolling-off is supreme (see p. 18). For many years a similar ceremony has obtained for men called out to the home work: and in recent times a special ceremony has been devised for all men going out at the end of the summer term.

Richmond honours, too, the memory of her sons who have passed to their reward, in an Annual Service of Remembrance. A feature recently added is an occasion for farewell speeches and impressions of their College course, given by outgoing men, at the end of the summer term.

Dr. Waterhouse contributes elsewhere a general account of the studies. The outline of the time-table is what would generally be expected—rising-bells, breakfast and prayers, lectures, and afternoon free, and study during the evenings in preparation for the next day. James Lewis writes of olden days: 'We lived a Spartan life—up before 6 a.m., and in our studies by six. Lights out at 10 p.m. and off to bed—and no smoking!' D. M. Rowland's cartoon (opposite) is an amusing commentary on the daily scheme. A large bell hung on the staircase now replaces the 'peripatetic' ones. G. Kellett Grice says that in his day the bell had a text on it: 'Art thou come to torment me before the time?'

The devotional life is nourished in all possible ways. Men are out preaching on Sundays, either supplying pulpits over the south of England or at their 'mission-band' chapels; men who are free will attend morning service at the College Chapel, and hear the famous preachers at the centre of things in the evening. Morning Prayers are taken by all in turn, formerly in the large lecture-room, and, since the rebuilding, in the College Chapel. There are prayer meetings as frequently as possible; the day has varied through the years, but the purpose is the same. The weekly preaching service is sometimes a means of grace, and always an ordeal to the student whose turn it is to conduct it, and to receive kindly tutorial criticism and advice afterwards. Since 1926 there has been a Saturday morning Communion Service, and very gracious memories are mine of Dr. Church's ministrations at those quiet services. Friday nights are devoted alternately to class meetings and to speakers from the outside world. Once a term there is a 'Quiet Day' to which there have come such speakers as Miss Evelyn Underhill, or some son of Richmond, like Leslie Weatherhead. From 1938 a Saturday noon prayer meeting was held for world peace, at which French, English, and German students have gathered. The College is silent between 10.30 and 11 p.m.

Sports life has always been vigorous, and often very successful. It was not always so, and an article contributed by George Fletcher to an old magazine recalls that cricket started in Petersham Park round about 1858, being spoken of as 'tupto'. Previously, at both Didsbury and Richmond games were frowned upon.[1] Our fathers knew nothing of a day when a Richmond man would captain the London University football team, as did D. M. Jones in 1931. It is difficult to imagine their comments on an entry in the Students' Minutes, whereby 2s. 6d. was granted to Mr. F. Robins (the present cheerful and willing 'College Engineer') 'for extraction of a tooth lost when refereeing a College football match'! And had they seen a Tutor in New Testament Literature walking back to the base-line of a tennis court with the quietest air, after despatching an opponent with an impossible return! . . . In 1932 the College won all three shields of the London Theological League—football, cricket, and tennis.

We have hinted at the far-reaching effects of the life of man with man at Richmond and have spoken of the 'tea-clubs'. Other unofficial meetings have always been popular —little gatherings for yarning and tea-drinking until late into the night. Afternoons are free for walks, and there are outings to Town. The 'den tea' has been for long now a popular institution as a means of entertaining friends or family—and very charming a tea-table can look in those low-windowed studies with their creeper-covered walls and the bright green of the lawns and gardens beyond.

While the energies of the men are pretty fully extended on the studies comprised in the College course, there is a wise cultivation of wider interests which they will come across in

[1] Fifty years ago, voices in the Tutors' meeting declared 'Football is of the devil!' See letter in *Methodist Recorder*, January 23, 1863.

their ministry. Students always appear at Fellowship of the Kingdom and other conferences, such as the Swanwick Music Conference. Opportunities for special courses, such as those for child study and youth work, etc., are greater now than ever they were, and men are given courses, sometimes lasting a year, at other schools and colleges. The Rev. F. Clifford Taylor gave regular lectures on Sunday-school method for some years prior to the war. The Tutors have always been very kind in delivering 'Saturday lectures' on subjects outside the curriculum; Dr. Waterhouse on 'Heredity' and Dr. Ryder Smith on the Hymn-book, are instances that come readily to mind. For some years before the war there was an exchange system with Marburg University, in Germany, and the presence of the German students (in at least one case a 'red-hot Nazi'!) has certainly made for interest, while two of the Richmond men have returned with German doctorates in their 'bag'.

On the cultural side there are the Friday-night meetings. The men send requests for speakers to the Governor—the list is of a highly exalted nature, usually being subsequently whittled down to the limits of at least remote possibilities! On one occasion Keir Hardie was asked for and the Governor besought the men *with tears* not to press the request! Studdert Kennedy came in 1926 for such a talk. At the time of Parliamentary elections, the candidates or their representatives have come to address the men. Debating societies have risen and fallen through the years, never with remarkable success. The most recent effort was in 1940, and the Minutes of the Society lay it down that 'parliamentary language' is to be used. The brightest event in the life of this recent revival seems to have been a debate with Southlands: 'That romantic ideas of love are a hindrance to the formation of a successful marriage'! The latest 'cultural' society sprang up in 1941—the 'Heliconian Society'. But such societies have always come and gone—there is a spirited account of some in *R.A.C.*, an old magazine. In earlier days (says Mr. Gregory Harris) there was the office of the College Poet, who was expected to produce 'a screed of verses' on any notable occasion. We have his dirge-like chant on the death of 'John Wesley', the College donkey, which begins:

*'Dead is the beast that bore our Founder's glorious name |,
The College grounds no more his services shall claim |'*

Relations with the Staff are nowadays very pleasant and amiable; the House Governor holds the useful office of mediator, invariably with success. The most historic instance of clash between Tutors and students occurred when Hugh Price Hughes denounced the segregation of missionary students.[1] But though the minute of the Discipline Committee reads fiercely enough in recording this, the end of it was mercy. Four years later, the Discipline Committee took action which the men apparently regarded as severe, and they presented a 'memorial'. In dismissing it, the Committee, declare that they 'cannot but express strong disapprobation of the practice of sending such memorials. The Committee entertains still stronger objection to the practice of holding meetings of the students collectively, to consider and review the exercise of discipline in the Institution, as such meetings must necessarily interfere with the harmonious working of the Institution, and cannot be reconciled with our rules and usages'. 'Our usages' were apparently comprised in the sentiment: 'Theirs not to reason why. . . .' Yet there are many kindly touches, as in the case of the student who resigned, 'being discouraged through grievous failure in the examinations'. The Committee persuaded him to try again, though he did resign three months later.

Said John Farrar in 1845: 'In cases where kindly admonition may have been deemed requisite it has been received with thankful submission.' (More is there than meets the eye; and many a man has been thankful all the days of his life for a quiet word known to none other in his tutor's study.)

The crest of the College (reproduced on the title-page) is that of the Wesley family, and dates from 1321-4. The motto is different, however—*Pro Christo et Ecclesia*, adopted in 1911.

[1] P. 23.

The war-cry consists of the famous words of Pheidippides after Marathon: 'O fellow citizens, rejoice. We conquer!' The full College colours are purple (London University), white (theology), red, and green; the present blazer is maroon, with narrow green stripes. The College song is adapted from verses written in 1925 by Reginald Glanville, with music by R. W. Debenham Peck, and was adopted in 1931.

Some account of the College magazines may be of interest. It is difficult to decide when the first appeared. Writing in the *Eleusinian*, Albert Clayton mentioned the *Anchorite*, a manuscript journal, published on Saturday mornings around 1861 or so. About 1886-9 the *Journal of the Scientific Society of Richmond College* and the *R.C. Literary and Scientific Journal* seem to have flourished; and I have found a reference to what may possibly be magazines called *Chin* and *Gas* (!) about this time. Round about 1898 there appeared a spirited publication known as the *Flashlight*. It was prepared on a duplicator of the 'jellygraph' variety, and it was edited, says Dr. Waterhouse, by a small committee, but the contributions were anonymous, with the purpose of avoiding assault, for the *Flashlight* was scurrilously personal! Reading these faded pages, one can but agree with Dr. Waterhouse. We read that Joshua Hoyle was a super-efficient Monitor; there is a displayed advertisement, 'Dull wits sharpened', by one W. F. Lofthouse (more in this than meets the eyes). 'Favourite poems' appear, which the Editor professes to have collected from various students, including the favourite poem of 'Hydor oikos'.[1]

The first printed magazine was the *Eleusinian*, edited by Arthur Walters in 1901. It started auspiciously with good wishes from Tutors, from Hugh Price Hughes, Marshall Hartley, and others of the great. The first number contained a memorial to Queen Victoria, and the announcement of E. S. Waterhouse's B.A. George Jackson also appears, urging men to make it their solemn vow that they will live for their pulpit, adding that of statesmen and administrators and the like 'a few is enough!'

[1] Only too evidently a reference to the present Principal.

Dr. Waterhouse has said[1] that the *Eleusinian* died of excessive respectability; but this cannot be said of *R.A.C.* (Round About College), which followed in 1906. This again was produced by 'jellygraph', and rather confirms one's impression that print was needed for a properly successful magazine. An article called 'My Impressions of the First Year' occupies two pages out of the brief twelve, and omits nothing that is scarifying on this enticing subject.

The present magazine, *The Old Chariot*, appeared in 1911, and with gaps, occasionally considerable, has continued to this day. A perusal of the whole series leaves one with the reflection that there is nothing new under the sun; generations of students follow one another in making fun out of the same ingredients, the Tutors and the studies finding high place in this category. The magazine has become lighter with the years (though a fairly recent number bestows six pages out of twenty-six on a formidable article entitled 'God and the Absolute').

Occasional references in this volume to the 'Mission Bands' may be rounded off by a brief description of this valuable work. Every student is appointed to one or other of the Bands, which consist of about six men, under a 'bishop'; and to this Band is mainly committed the preaching, and to some extent the immediate pastoral oversight, of a London church. Such Bands have also assisted at Central Halls, and at the College Chapel. The experience thus gained is exceedingly valuable. Two men will normally visit their church each Sunday, in the intervals of 'supply' preaching in many pulpits over the South of England.

And so, with these impressions of the many-sided life of Richmond, we may take our leave of 'this building with its echoing corridors and heights, precious with a thousand memories of midnight songs, of quiet talks, high hopes and deep resolves' (Richmond 'General Tradition').

[1] In an interesting article on the College magazines, *Old Chariot*, No. 9, p. 11.

EPILOGUE

LIKE all the world, Richmond is in war-dress to-day.

The first sign of war changes is observed as we pass No. 30 Friar's Stile Road. No chance to-day of greeting the dapper, kindly figure of the Tutor in New Testament languages. A wide opening has been made by the side of the College Chapel for the use of Civil Defence motors, and the shrubbery has become an asphalt yard: the Chapel itself has become a repository for the furniture from ruined houses. (Only those whom war has left mainly untouched will fail to see here a work of mercy; the Chapel's use had been suspended through the difficulties of the time. A notice refers visitors to the Chapel in the College for a morning service.)

So we proceed along Friar's Stile Road, turning left by the tea-shop, recently very smartly painted to attract the uniformed and other visitors to the town. On the new gateway of the College, looking down the Avenue, there is a notice which surely brings pride to a Richmond man: 'University of London, Temporary Administrative Headquarters.' This is the capital of the University—surely an ideal arrangement for these troubled years.

The Avenue needs remetalling. But, ye riders of cycles, it nearly always did! The football field is under cultivation. Here So-and-So scored his goal; here the doughty —— was centre-half. To-day the field, turned over by a land-girl with a motor-plough, produces vegetables instead.

The College looks the same at the end of the long Avenue. Yes, as we turn the curve of the path, where Garden Party tickets were sold in happier days, all looks much the same. . . . As we look more precisely across the front of the College, however, there are certain differences. Was that a girl looking out from a Lower Chequers window? One of the University staff, of course. And the flower beds are being prepared for vegetables. But a brave bed of polyanthuses gleams by the front doorway.

Alas for the glory of the pinnacled front! Blast and 'near misses' have brought down many a spire. They lie in an ordered heap under the Prayer Room windows. The Principal lives yonder still, but there are no men; and he has charge of a church in Richmond Circuit, in addition to the still considerable duties of the College, for it must be kept in readiness for the days after the war.

Here and there you will see a land-girl, working deftly at the College gardens under the charge of the redoubtable Mr. Brixton.

If you are on Richmond business, you may still make your way into the basement, and at the end of the new broad corridor where are the Games Room and Common Room you will discern a real A.R.P. post, complete with all personnel, telephonists, and the rest. The Games Room is silent; the Common Room the same; all blacked-out with heavy curtains. Books from the Lycett Room, in carefully marked packing-cases, line the Common Room walls; and here in piled boxes the careful College Secretary has stored the College papers against the day when the storm ends.

And before they went, this last generation did a thing that moves us. They wrote of Richmond,[1] that those who come may know the old ways which we loved. Their words shall end this picture:

'Many of these Traditions', they say, 'have been handed down from the earliest days; and all of them, with the general routine, have become sacred to those of us who love this place. For these traditions, offices and rules have proved an effective means to the deepest fellowship many of us have ever known.

'We therefore pass them on to you in the confidence that you will take this torch from our hands, and maintain the continuity of all that is best in the life and spirit of Richmond.'

So truly do we all, men of old Richmond, speak to the new

[1] Pp. 31, 148.

generation that shall come eagerly, as we all came, to learn and to be moulded, to receive the guidance that showed us how to do our work. So we all join, and you who come after us will join too, in adoration of our God, in gratitude to Richmond, our mother.

ω ΣΥΜΠΟΛΙΤΑΙ ΧΑΙΡΕΤΕ ΝΙΚωΜΕΝ

E. W. Tattersall

RICHMOND

E. W. Tattersall

THE ENTRANCE HALL

A CORNER OF THE LIBRARY

DAVID HILL
1861

HUGH PRICE HUGHES
1865

THE TUTORS

House Governor

From 1910, 'Resident Tutor, with charge of the Institution House' (now called 'College House'). From 1888 the Governor also taught 'Pastoral Theology and Church Organization' (now called 'Church History'); and until 1910 a note was added '... shall also be Governor and have Pastoral Charge of the Students' (see p. 95).

S. indicates Secretary of Conference.
P. indicates President of Conference.

1843–6.	Philip C. Turner.
1846–8.	W. W. Stamp (*P.*, 1860)
1848–55.	S. Jackson (*P.*, 1847)
1855–8.	W. M. Harvard
1858–68.	Alfred Barrett
1868–91.	Daniel Sanderson
1891–1909.	George Fletcher
1909–15.	T. H. Barratt
1920–9.	W. T. A. Barber (Pastoral Theology and—for one year—Comparative Religion) *P.*, 1919
1929–35.	Leslie F. Church (Pastoral Theology and Church History) *P.*, 1943
1935–41.	S. G. Dimond

Theology

1843–61.	Thos. Jackson (*P.*, 1838, 1849)
1861–8.	John Lomas (*P.*, 1853)
1868–85.	George Osborn (*P.*, 1863, 1881)
1885–1905.	J. Agar Beet
1905–15.	W. T. Davison (*P.*, 1901)
1920–40.	C. Ryder Smith (*P.*, 1931)
1940–	Harold Roberts

Biblical Literature and Classics

1843–57.	John Farrar (*S.*, 1851–3, 1859–69; *P.*, 1854, 1870)

1857–68. Benjamin Hellier
1868–74. W. F. Moulton (*P.*, 1890)
1875–81. F. P. Napier and G. G. Findlay
1881–3. F. P. Napier and W. T. Davison
1883–91. W. T. Davison (Classical Tutor, 1883–4; Biblical Literature and Classics, 1885–6; Biblical Literature and Exegesis, 1887–91) *P.*, 1901
1887–91. J. G. Tasker (Classics and Mathematics) *P.*, 1916
1891–1915. Alfred S. Geden (Biblical Literature and Exegesis and Classics, 1891–1904; Old Testament Language and Literature and Classics, 1904–15)
1904–10. J. A. Vanes (New Testament Language and Literature and Philosophy)
1910–15. Harry Bisseker (New Testament Language and Literature and Philosophy)
1920– F. Bertram Clogg (New Testament Language and Literature and Classics)

Philosophy

See Biblical Literature and Classics for period before 1920.

1920– E. S. Waterhouse

Principal

Title first used in 1910; see p. 95.

1910–20. W. T. Davison (*P.*, 1901)
1920–9. W. T. A. Barber (*P.*, 1919)
1929–40. C. Ryder Smith (*P.*, 1931)
1940– E. S. Waterhouse

Assistant Tutors

1847–51. J. D. Geden
1851–53. Robert Newton Young (*S.*, 1881–5; *P.*, 1886)
1854–55. William Gibson
1858–68. W. F. Moulton (*P.*, 1890)
1868–72. Marshall Hartley (*S.*, 1895–1902); *P.*, 1903
1871–6. James Cooling
1872–5. F. P. Napier
1874–5. G. G. Findlay
1876–80. J. G. Tasker (*P.*, 1916)

1880-2. W. H. Findlay
1882-4. W. T. A. Barber (*P.*, 1919)
1884-7. J. G. Tasker (*P.*, 1916)
1886-9. F. W. Kellett
1889-91. E. O. Barrett
1891-3. W. Percy Hutton
1891-4. Thos. Stephenson
1893-6. Harold C. Morton
1894-6. James H. Darrell
1896-8. C. F. Hunter
1896-8. Wm. F. Lofthouse (*P.*, 1929)
1898-1904. Thos. Stephenson

1902-4. Percy M. Wright
1904-6. Ernest G. Loosley
1906-9. R. Idwal Hopwood
1909-12. F. Bertram Clogg
1912-15. Conrad Skinner
1915-16. Wm. H. Dyson[1]
1920-5. H. D. Anthony
1925-8. Stanley R. Hayward
1928-30. J. T. Jones
1930-2. A. Marcus Ward
1931-2. Kenneth G. Bloxham
1932-7. Geo. E. Cornforth
1937-9. C. F. Davey
1939- Geo. W. Anderson

TABLE OF SENIORITY

1874
T. Fuller Bryant

1875
Richard Rossall

1876
Thomas Little
George Marris
William J. Pearce

1877
Charles Bone

1880
J. G. Wheatcroft Brown
Ebenezer Jolliffe

1881
John England
Frederick A. Smith
John Williams (A)

1882
Alfred S. Sharp

1883
J. Wesley Davies
J. Courtenay James
Alfred J. Norman
Franklyn G. Smith
John Williams (B)

1884
Walter Charlesworth
Charles Feneley
Richard Hall
William H. Hart
Sheldon Knapp
John Moffatt
John H. Willington

[1] Killed in action, 1916; appointed, but never served.

COLLEGE OFFICIALS FROM 1912
(*No earlier details*)

	Chairman	*Vice-Chairman*	*Secretary*
1912.	C. Edgar James	—	Norman E. Dando
1913.	C. Gordon Early	S. Magor	Ernest P. Picken
1914.	Bert Adcock	G. W. Alway	J. H. Price
		Herbert Phelps	H. Stanley Southall
			T. Stanley Cannon
1915.	Leslie D. Weatherhead	J. M. Darlington	E. C. Horler
1920.	H. V. Shepherd	A. Salmon	L. W. Juby
1921.	H. V. Shepherd	T. R. Foulger	W. Horner
	T. R. Foulger	J. Rees	—
1922.	T. R. Foulger	H. Buxton	E. H. Lawrence
1923.	J. Leslie Webb	R. Chaloner	C. G. Baker
1924.	J. Leslie Webb	R. Glanville	A. Powell Davies
1925.	A. T. Johns	A. Kingsley Lloyd	Cecil H. G. Carter
1926.	Kenneth H. Crosby	A. T. Johns	R. Leslie Waterman
1927.	F. E. Christmas	W. J. Barrett	A. G. Payne
1928.	E. A. P. Attwater	Arnold Pendlebury	R. J. Brown
1929.	Wilfred Easton	R. B. Wright	M. A. Clarke
1930.	Kenneth G. Bloxham	E. B. Wright	Frank Cumbers
1931.	A. J. Stanbury	E. R. Sarchet	H. J. Martin
		A. R. Burch	
1932.	T. J. Foinette	T. F. Glasson	L. M. Thompson
1933.	Percy Scott	E. W. Funnell	Eric G. Chapman
1934.	A. B. Jones	Levi Dawson	T. L. Thexton
1935.	T. L. Thexton	K. E. Jinks	Howard A. Trevis
1936.	Maldwyn O. Williams	Leonard E. White	P. Stewart May
1937.	Allan H. Currey	W. H. Marchant	H. Richmond Stuart
1938.	S. Clive Thexton	E. T. Scott	P. Napier Milne
1939.	K. J. Payne	W. P. D. Morley	K. S. Armitstead
1940.	B. Arthur Shaw	E. G. Green	Kenneth Underwood
1941.	Kenneth Underwood	—	S. C. Fittall

RECORDS

LIST OF STUDENTS, 1843-1940

1843

Thomas Adams
Henry Balls
David Barley
William Binks
Abel Burgess
Samuel Burrell
Benjamin Chapman
John W. Davies
Geo. H. Davis
George Deery
William Edwards
Richard Eland
Edwin Fice
Benjamin Field
Matthew Giles
Thomas B. Glanville
Richard Hardy
Thomas H. Hill
John Hodson
Joseph Jackson
John Livingstone
John McKenny
John F. Moody
Joseph Morris
Joshua Mottram
Henry Needle
Wm. T. Nelson
Geo. Parkinson
John Pascoe
Felix H. Pickworth
Henry Ramin
Robert Rees
John Roberts
Geo. Smith
Geo. C. Taylor
Michael C. Taylor
John Thomas
Anthony Ward
Jabez B. Waterhouse
John Wesley Wilson
Joseph Wright

1844

George Alton
Samuel Coley
William Cuttle
Frederick F. Edmunds
Samuel Ferguson
John Dury Geden
David Griffiths
Benjamin Hellier
Henry Pope
William Morley Punshon (*P.*, 1874)
Edward J. Robinson
John Skidmore
John Walton
James H. Wayte
Charles Willis

1845

John Wesley Close
Joseph Fletcher
Frederick Hart
William Horton
John Jones
Henry Keet
Joseph Oram
Charles Potts
William Shaw
Joseph Sutton
Charles Williams

1846

Thomas Chope
Edward Collier
James M. Cranswick
John Elam
Walter P. Garry
Elias Geake
Geo. Hodgson
Alexander T. James
David Jones
John Lesson
Henry Pollinger
Richard Smetham
John Wood

1847

Thomas Akroyd
Joseph Bate
John Brown
Henry Cattle
Jas. D. Dodgson
John Tait Duncan
Chas. Garrett
John Gilbert
Fredk. C. Haime
Ebenezer Hewlett
William Hill
John Jeffreys
James F. Masters
Joshua Mason
Chas. M. Merry
Marmaduke C. Osborn (*S.*, 1878–80)
Chas. S. Parsons
Joseph Posnett
Joseph Rippon
James Smith
Samuel Underwood
Saml. Vaughan
John Webb
Joseph Willis

1848

William R. Beach
Emile F. Cook
Jonathan Dale
Theophilus Lessey
Henry Parry
John Polglase
Alexander Reid
Walter Tregellas
Joseph Williams
Henry P. Wilson

1849

Thomas M. Albrighton
J. Coultas
Walter P. Johns
Samuel Pritchard
Lionel Reay
John Rhodes
Joseph H. Rylance
Humphrey M. Wightwick

1850

George Osborn Bate
James H. Bishop
Thomas Brackenbury
Charles Burgant
Joseph Bush
John Cooper
Edwin Cox
Josiah Cox
William T. Davies
William Dodsworth
Wm. H. W. Evans
John S. Fordham
Charles Hoskins
Featherstone Kellett
William Pepperell
Samuel Radcliffe
William N. Richard
Richard Taylor
Theophilus Taylor
John Vercoe
William Wilson
Samuel Wray
Robert Newton Young (*S.*, 1881–5; *P.*, 1886)

1851

Samuel Hutton
Henry Pimm
John Preston
Wm. O. Simpson
Samuel J. Smith
Edward D. Webb

1852

Henry R. Burton
Edward Day
William H. Dean
William H. Dyson
Ebenezer Evans
John Greathead
Robert W. Pordidge
James S. H. Royce
John Scott
Harrison Waddington
Abraham S. White

1853

John Bell
Samuel H. Morton

1854

Wm. Clarke
Wm. Holford
George G. Huxtable
Ben. Oliel
Thomas Protheroe
Thomas Raspass

1855

Benjamin Broadley
Wm. R. C. Cockill
James H. Cummings
Thomas Clulow
James Greenland
Jabez Iredale
John Jones
Geo. H. Smith
Henry J. Sykes
Silas E. Symons

1856

Henry Andrews
Wm. Alnwick
W. Wm. Calladine
Mark Davenport
Henry Douthwaite
Caleb Foster
Thomas Jarrett
John S. Parkes
Daniel Pearson
Wm. Page Roberts
Wm. Spilsbury
Thomas E. Treffry
David J. Waller (*S.*, 1886–94; *P.*, 1895)

1857

Frederick Ewer
John Harris
Edwin Hillier
Arthur B. Holford
John G. Morrow
Samuel Sheard
Joseph Start Strangeways
George Terry
Anthony G. Ward

1858

Thomas Baine
James R. Berry
Thomas W. Blanshard
William Brewins
James H. Broadbent
Wesley Brunyate
Edward Dodds
Geo. Fletcher
George Fryar
Thomas Gane
George Gibson

1858—*cont.*

John Harris
John E. Hicks
Hy. G. Highfield
Thomas Hubbard
James Langley
Thomas H. Leale
John Mackintosh
Jacob Marratt
Joseph Milligan
John M. Morrell
Thomas Morris
Joseph Nettleton
Charles B. Pattison
Zadok Robinson
Jeremiah Sackett
Thomas Stephenson
T. Bowman Stephenson (*P.*, 1891)
David Stewart
Francis Tait
Francis Truman
Wm. Walton
Wm. L. Watkinson (*P.* 1897)
Joseph White

1859

John Allsopp
Geo. Backhouse
George Baugh
Robert Bentley
Charles Brighouse
Noah Cooke
Samuel Dalzell
Thomas Delbridge
James Fish
John Greenwood
Henry Hughes
Wm. Masking
Wm. Henry Massey
James Nicholson
Saml. Normington
Abraham Pearce
Newton R. Penny
Wm. Rayner
Thomas Robson
Charles C. Rorke
James Sawtell
John Stephenson
Alfred Taylor
John Drayton Thomas

1860

Josiah Banham
John R. Bennett
James Berry
John Browne
Robert Burdon
William H. Charlesworth
Wm. H. Dallinger
Henry E. Henry
Henry Hornby
Josiah Hudson
John Kirby
John Lamplough
S. Wesley Lawton
Henry Little
John Arthur Lyth
James Napoleon Manning
Hugh Reid McGahie
William Nicholson
Charles Olden
Henry Parkes
Thomas Peers
Geo. Robinson
Thomas Rowson
Geo. Scott
Luke Scott
William Seed
Richard Sellors
Elisha M. Shearn
Robert G. Smith
S. Horner Stott
Geo. H. Thompson
John H. Walthen
George T. Watts
Charles Wiles
Henry Woodhouse

1861

G. Lupton Allen
Thos. Ayrton

RICHMOND COLLEGE 167

Samuel F. Balch
George G. Ballard
John Bourne
Joseph M. Browne
Wm. Burchell
Wm. Caldecott
Henry L. Carr
Winterly Crouch
Benjamin Dixon
Evan Evans
Thomas Hare
David Hill
J. Hollingshead
James M'Turk
Charles D. Newman
Joel Peters
H. Owen Rattenbury
John C. Reddaway
Thomas Roberts
Francis B. Sandbach
Wm. Scarborough
William Spenseley
Jabez B. Stephenson
David Wright
Buckley Yates
James Yeames

1862

Manasseh Barker
Joseph Agar Beet
Thomas Bolam
Theo. Chubb
Albert Clayton (*P.*, 1906)
Edwin Dixon
John Evans
John W. Evans
Albert Fentiman
John Gardiner
Joseph Gibson
William Glanville
Matthew Grimmer
John H. Grubb
Richard Hayes
Frederick Hunter
John Jackson
John Jenkin

John S. Ladd
John Newell
Thomas H. Penrith
Peter W. Ramsden
James Robertson
William Robinson
John H. Rogers
Enoch Salt
William D. L. Slack
Joseph S. Silcox
Joseph Spence
George F. Swinnerton
James Walter
Samuel R. Williams

1863

James Bransom
Joseph Broadbent
Thomas Broadbent
J. Milton Brown
Francis Chapman
William E. Codling
Charles O. Eldridge
Henry S. Elvins
Edward S. Evans
Isaac Harding
Joshua Hawkins
Thomas H. Horrell
Matthew S. Horton
Wm. C. Lawry
George Lester
William J. Lewis
Edward P. Lowry
John Marquand
Frederick P. Napier
John Osborn
Matthew H. Parkinson
John Otley Rhodes
James Rogers
Stephen G. Scott
Frederick Holmes Smith
Ralph M. Spoor
Stephen Sutton
Robert Thomas
J. Norton Vine
Henry W. Watkins

1863—*cont.*

Owen Watkins
Silvester Whitehead (*P.*, 1904)
Jabez Wilson
Thomas Worthington

1864

John W. Atkinson
Thomas Austin
Joseph Bale
Edward S. Banham
J. Holland Brown
Henry Bone
John Burdon
Wesley Button
Richard S. Campbell
John Cassie
J. Surman Cooke
Sydney J. P. Dunman
Geo. R. Graham
Wm. H. Groves
George Hack
Jas. S. Hill
Thomas J. Kent
John Martin
Robert H. Moreton
James Morrow
Thomas Neill
Geo. Oyston
Andrew Palmer
Patrick Pizey
Wm. Russell
W. Darlow Sarjeant
Jacob Stephenson
Geo. S. Stoker
Joseph Symes
Henry Watts

1865

Joseph B. Alger
Edward Bowman
Richard Brown
Edward Burton
James W. Carr

John Crump
Robert Culley
Alex. F. Fogwell
James C. Fowler
Edwin Goodhall
Charles Harris
Thomas B. Harrowell
Alfred Hewitt
George Hinson
Hugh Price Hughes (*P.*, 1898)
Alfred Llewellyn
Arthur J. O. Lyle
Alfred Martyn
J. Hawkins Pawlyn
Thomas G. Selby
George E. Sheers
Joseph Shrimpton
Samuel L. Smith
William Stevinson
William S. D. Winter

1866

Robert A. Bilkey
Theodore Bishop
Samuel T. Bosward
James C. Brewer
Philip Callier
Ebenezer Cole
John Curtis
Frederick C. Dugdale
William Dunstan
John Dymond
Alexander English
Josiah Evans
Wm. Halstead
Thomas Jenkin
Silas Jones
John Law
John Leal
John Leathley
Frederick M. Lowry
William Martin
Josiah Mee
Robert Passmore
W. Allen Phillips
Henry J. Quilter

Alfred Sargant
Joseph F. Southern
John Shipstone
Robert Tebb
Wm. G. Thomas

1867

Amos Armitage
James Bolton
J. Reeves Brown
Joseph H. Cadman
Henry W. Catton
John Crawshaw
John F. Davis
Edward De Courcy
John R. Dickson
John Filstead
John C. W. Gostick
Marshall Hartley (*S.*, 1895–1902; *P*, 1903)
John Kennings
Thomas Lear
J. Powell Lowe
John Mead
James Monahan
James Parker
William Parker
John T. Patey
Joseph Robinson
Jas. Bennett Sharp
E. Stanley Shelton
Alfred J. Silcox
Thomas P. Spencer
Wm. A. Templar
H. Epworth Thompson
John Turner
John W. Woodliffe

1868

Mortimer Allen
Charles Angwin
Josephus Bishop
Thomas Blackett
Edward D. Dannatt
Wm. H. Evans

Edward Gibbens
John T. F. Halligey
Thomas Hosking
William Jackson
John J. Lewis
Ezekiel Lones
Charles Pickels
Thomas R. Picot
Thomas Rae
Joseph Rhodes
Edward Jas. Rodd
Jeremiah Sanson
Gardener Scates
David H. Shankland
Joseph Simpson
Archibald Taylor
Wm. Geo. Taylor
John H. Trevenen
Wm. J. Williams
John P. Wright

1869

Enoch Biscombe
George Bond
R. Starling Boulter
John W. Brewer
Thomas G. Carr
Arthur Payne Chaplin
James Cooling
Richard W. Cusworth
Frederick Elton
James Etchells
Geo. G. Findlay
C. Hale Hocken
Francis W. Isitt
John Jeffery
Richard Lloyd Jones
William T. Jones
Charles E. Le Feaux
Edwin T. Lewis
Solomon Matthews
T. Frederick Nicholson
John G. Pearson
C. F. Richardson
Alfred P. Riddett
Charles Rose

1869—cont.

Philip Sadler
George M. Slade
J. Crompton Sowerbutts
Frederick Henry Thomas
George Weavind
Alfred S. Williams
John E. Winter

John Enoch Parsonson
Edward Pyle
Alfred T. Rhodes
Thomas Roper
Thomas Sanderson
Oswald Welch
Charles T. Williams

1870

George Adcock
Samuel B. Cawood
William Ellis
John Wesley George
Samuel Goodyer
James Green
Frederic Bibby Hargreaves
Samuel Langdon
John Hardy Lyth
Benjamin John Meek
John Milum
John J. Parker
Jabez Bunting Portrey
Joseph Race
James Troubridge Satchell
Edward Sinzininex
Robert Whittleton
Samuel R. Wilkin
John S. Williams

1872

Wm. J. Baker
John W. Bell
Thomas Bramfitt
Jonathan Chapple
Paul Clipsham
Hy. J. Cornish
Thos. S. Dyson
Hampson J. Eckersley
James Fieldhouse
Henry Haigh (*P.*, 1911)
Frederick Halliday
Edward Harris
J. D. Hennessey
R. Hornabrook
Arthur H. Male
Arthur W. Nightingale
William Penrose
Robert Simpson
John Thompson
William S. Tomlinson
Michael Westcombe
John Wilson

1871

Henry Adams
Elijah Bew
Arthur Bourne
Fredk. S. Chesters
William H. Farnell
John B. Gedye
George Grayson
Thomas Hammond
William Markwick
Edward Martin
Frederic James Masters

1873

William Allen
Arthur Attewell
Joseph R. Broadhead
Philip J. Cocking
William F. Cocks
William Dowson
George Dyer
Jonathan Grant
Chas. M. Greenway

John E. Howard
David Huddlestone
John Kernick
Luke Parr
George Patterson
Peter Presswell
Samuel F. Prior
Clement S. Reader
David A. Rees
William H. Rogers
E. Hudson Scott
Edwin R. Slack
Westmore S. Smith
John G. Tasker (*P.*, 1916)
Hugh H. Teague
Wm. W. Thackray
William Wall
William H. Williams

1874

William H. Atkin
Thomas H. Bailey
Walter T. Baker
John T. Bennett
Benjamin Bransom
T. Fuller Bryant
Thomas A. Chalker
William Cliff
E. Doddrell
Hilderic Friend
J. Jackson
Edward Jope
Henry Lamb
J. Lock
John R. Newall
Charles Pettman
J. Povah
Edwin Seller
James Sharp
Arthur Shipham
Richard Smith
Edward Strutt
John M. Thompson
Joseph Whitney
Thomas H. Wilkin

1875

Chas. F. Braithwaite
Frederick B. Cowl
Wm. Dawson
Wm. M. Douglas
John S. Fordham
William J. Hacker
Wm. C. Kendall
James A. D. J. Macdonald
Robt. W. L. Mansfield
Robert Matterson
Frederick O. Miller
John Pickup
Richard Rossall
John D. Scott
John W. Shrimpton
John W. Simpson
Robert Simpson
John R. Slater
George C. Trimmer
Fredk. Tunbridge
Frank Turner
Ellis J. Williams

1876

Samuel Arnold
W. Terry Coppin
Henry Cotton
Evan Davies
John Dugdale
James Ellis
Alfred Farrar
Harvey Field
Richard Garbett
Geo. B. Glover
Frederick W. Gostick
John Grimshaw
Josiah W. Harbord
Marmaduke Hare
Grainger Hargreaves
Robert Heslam
Richard Hill
Samuel Hill
J. Griffin Hodson
George J. Holman

1876—*cont.*

Tom Ivens
Edward H. Jackson
James Jenkin
Owen Morgan Jones
Wm. Owen Jones
Thomas Little
George Marris
Richard Morgan
William J. Pearce
Jacob Pritchard
George Rayner
John P. Roberts
Benjamin Robinson
Simon Snowdon
William Taggart
Henry Thomas
William J. Weare
Frederick M. Webster
Joseph H. Wilsdon
Herbert J. Wonfor

Marshall Limon
T. E. Marsh
J. G. Martin
George D. Mason
Thos. E. North
H. Pennington
I. Perry
W. H. Jackson Picken
Wm. Powell
Benjamin Pratt
John Price
W. Titcombe Pullen
Samuel H. Ravenscroft
Wm. Rosewarne
Rowland Rowlands
W. Marshman Spencer
Charles L. Tabraham
A. Taylor
J. C. Warner
J. B. Wilkin
Henry Williams
T. W. Winfield

1877

Nendick Abraham
John P. Back
William L. Bennett
C. H. Bishop
W. O. Bloomfield
Charles Bone
John W. Booth
Jabez Bridge
D. B. Bridgwood
James Bryant
Edward S. Burnett
Joseph Culshaw
George A. Currier
Robert Dixon
Frederick G. Elliott
Michael J. Elliott
John G. Emerson
J. B. Gratton
William R. Griffin
G. W. Jackson
D. James
Joseph Kewley

1878

W. H. Aspden
Alex. Atkinson
Wm. Baker
Geo. Wm. Baxter
Thos. Brackenbury
Arthur Brunt
Amos Burnet (*P.*, 1924)
Oliver Carey
George W. Clutterbuck
Charles Denham
J. K. Derry
John W. Faraday
J. H. Gathercole
W. E. Gillam
George Golightly
John W. Househam
Richard Jenkin
Robert W. Lewis
James W. Lord
Geo. Lowe
Joseph Parson
Wm. Pescod

W. C. Quiggin
Geo. Ed. Rowe
J. T. Smart
John Smith
Edwin J. Southall
Woodman Treleaven
Geo. E. Waterhouse

1879

W. J. Gregory Bestall
Thomas Cadman
Samuel Clark
Henry Wm. Davis
Paul Ellis
Wm. H. Findlay
William Goudie
William Greig
Jos. H. Hadley
Albert Hy. Hodges
Walter Lavender
Wm. Frank Martin
Jos. S. Masters
Joseph Metcalf
James Picot
Vivian Roberts
Thomas Spargo
James P. Taylor
S. George Tope
John Warrington
Harvey Wilkinson
James E. Wood

1880

James Banks
Thomas D. Barnes
Joseph G. Benson
J. G. Wheatcroft Brown
John Hy. Burnett
Wm. M. Cannell
James Cooke
Samuel Cooper
Thomas J. Drewett

Edward T. Dunstan
Ebenezer Edwards
J. A. Elliott[1]
H. Bramley Hart
Sydney R. Hodge
Jos. A. Johnson
Samuel J. Johnson
Ebenezer Jolliffe
Arthur T. Kinnings
Walter Lucas
Thomas Moscrop
Frederick T. Nicholson
Wm. Potts
Jos. B. Purnell
Thomas N. Robert
Geo. A. Theobald
Ebenezer J. M. Thomas
James W. Thompson
Thomas H. Wainman
Joseph West
Frederick C. Wright

1881

Wm. Bridie
M. Ferdinand Crewdson
John R. Ellis
John England
John Jabez Heal
Chas. Edward James
John Jones
Owen Jones
Ephraim Mortimer
Griffith W. Rogers
George Scates
Frederick A. Smith
John Wm. Smith
Edmund Tomlin
John Williams (A)

1882

Frederick Boden
Jesse Deacon

[1] Elliott's name is not included in any of the College records; but see *Minutes*, 1905.

1882—cont.

R. Hasell Killip
Aubrey L. Matson
Chas. Hy. Nield
Henry J. Parker
Wm. Priestnal
Arthur E. Restarick
William Rigby
Alfred S. Sharp
William Spink
William J. Underwood

1883

E. Wright Adcock
William Ashford
William Arthur Badger
Alfred T. R. Bartrop
E. Percy Blackburn
Edmund Bromage
Alfred H. Clegg
W. Arthur Cornaby
J. Wesley Davies
W. West Holdsworth
Richard Hughes
J. Courtenay James
Charles Samuel Lucas
George Lunn
Alfred J. Norman
Charles Rickard
Bryan Roe
Henry Scott
Isaac Shimmin
Franklyn G. Smith
Edward Charles Solomon
John Williams (B)

1884

Joseph H. Bateson
Arthur H. Bestall
Ralph Bradley
Fredk. J. Briscoe
Walter Charlesworth
Charles Feneley
W. Dyson Frater
James Goudie
Arthur Hall
Richard Hall
William H. Hart
Sheldon Knapp
John Moffatt
George W. Olver
John Onions
Gwilym Rees
Walter Sackett
H. Stanley Sandford
George S. Sheldon
J. Buckley Shute
W. Hunt Soper
John W. H. Stead
W. Stoyle
Arthur Triggs
J. Arthur Turner
John H. Willington
Edwin Woodward

1885

W. H. Adams
Wm. Baillie
A. Ernest Balch
John Barns
Thos. H. Boyd
A. W. Bishop
Andrew Bromwich
E. C. Chorley
J. Barnett Foster
G. E. Fox
A. M. Gliddon
Matthew Hall
Henry Hudson
George Jackson
Frank Jones
Ralph Philipson
Fredk. W. Kellett
Robert H. A. Morton
William C. J. Neville
E. E. Ormiston
J. Pendlebury
J. H. Samuel

William H. Sarchet
William Saywell
Edward J. Simons
F. H. Smith
F. N. Smith
J. Dawson Sutcliffe
C. H. Vine
E. J. Walkom
Robert J. Wardell
Richard Wormwell
J. E. Wright
Thos. E. Young

1886

John Bennetts
S. Parkes Cadman
John W. Colwell
J. Cullis Colwell
Francis Godson
W. Gregory Harris
John Howard
Geo. Charlton Hudson
Arthur E. Jones
F. H. Hooper Labbett
James Lewis
J. Henry Maddock
J. Scholefield Morris
Edwin Nicholson
Thomas W. Peeling
Wm. F. Penny
William C. Poles
Charles Ridge
Arthur Wm. Robins
Alfred B. Sackett
J. Roberts Saunders
Reuben R. Simons
Arthur Chinner Smith
Samuel R. B. Solomon
George Edward Startup
Benjamin Taylor
T. Morcom Taylor
Thomas Vaughan
Eben. Webster
Herbert Windross
Hy. James Marshall Withers

1887

Joshua Ainsworth
A. Andrews
George H. Armitage
William O. Barratt
W. A. Bird
Benjamin Crosby
J. Walker Duthie
W. Towers Garrett
J. Grubb
T. J. Hardy
J. Kimber Hill
Herbert A. Hodgson
S. W. Kay
George W. Kettleborough
E. Israel Lyndon
J. Oliver Mann
Albert C. Matthews
W. B. Milward
Alfred M. Morrow
Arthur W. Newboult
J. G. Oats
William H. Rolls
William Salisbury
Jos. Snell
John T. Tyerman
T. Warham
T. Featherstone Watson
David Williams
J. H. N. Williams
F. R. Wilson
Richard B. Woodward
Ernest H. Woolrych

1888

E. O. Barratt
G. H. Eva
Thomas C. Hillard
Charles R. Johnson
Ernest J. B. Kirtlan
T. S. Knowlson
W. H. A. Lee
M. J. Letcher
Samuel Marriott
W. A. Mellers

1888—cont.

Herbert Nicholls
J. Ash Parsons
J. S. Wesley Shrewsbury
Charles Speck
Allan Spencer
B. Spry
Percy Watchurst
J. Worthington

A. White
F. C. Woofenden

1889

Edward A. Bennett
Arthur W. Bunnett
Frank Cox
J. H. R. Douthwaite
Fredk. H. Harry
Peter P. Hazeley
C. Arnold Healing
C. J. H. Northcroft
Ernest W. Redfern
William R. Rice
C. Drayton Thomas
Cecil H. Wright

1890

J. C. Knight Anstey
James A. Archer
Thomas W. Bray
Henry J. Ellis
Albert L. Fillingham
A. Perry Gill
Alfred Hoad
Thos. Percy Hodgson
Frederick Lamb
R. Ernest Little
William Musson
Walter Norton
David D. Parnther
Franz Röth
Thomas Stephenson
C. E. Stocks
E. P. Thomas
Albert Ernest Vivian

1891

Arthur D. Baskerville
Walter Bell
Edwin Bottrill
W. Arthur Chettle
S. Leonard Evans
Richard W. Farnell
George R. Forde
Edward Greeves
J. Wesley Hughes
E. C. Jones
John Kelly
Herbert H. Minchin
Harold C. Morton
George L. Pullan
Joseph Reed
Sidney R. Rees
T. Charles Roberts
Wm. Francis Somerville
Henry Tregoning
Jas. Howard Wescott
J. Claude Whiting

1892

E. Stanley Edwards
Frank Edwards
Ernest F. Gedye
Frederick G. Howland
Charles E. Hutcheon
A. R. H. Ingram
Joseph Green Locke
Charles H. Monahan
Thomas Morris
Charles W. Posnett
R. Garrett Roberts
Robert Rogers
Wm. Foster Smith
John W. Stanlake
Robt. Taylor
C. Ensor Walters (*P.*, 1936)
Ralph H. Williams

RICHMOND COLLEGE

1893
Charles W. Annis
Wm. G. Bell
Charles R. Butcher
James H. Darrell
Christopher S. Chatterton
Austin H. Davey
James Davies
John Du Feu
Walter H. Dyer
Allworth Eardley
John S. Elmont
R. Moffatt Gautrey
Geo. C. Gould
David Hinchcliff
Wm. Hoad
Ebenezer J. Ives
William Looker
Herbert J. Philpott
E. Berwyn Roberts
Walter Seed
Charles H. Temple
Edgar W. Thompson
Owen S. Watkins
J. Colliver Williams

1894
Sidney J. Baker
James S. H. Bransome
Thomas A. Butcher
A. Trevellick Cape
William Eacott
Robert A. Ellis
Auguste Faure
Edmond Gounelle
Geo. Glandfield
R. Winboult Harding
Henry Highfield
Owen J. Letcher
John Lloyd
Henry Long
Richard P. Lowe
W. Gallaway Mitchell
Wm. Sherratt
W. Herbert Spencer

M

Ernest Titcomb
Albert Wood

1895
Anthony C. Baker
Edgar C. Barton
Edwin Brownscombe
C. Phillips Cape
Oliver J. Griffin
William Humphrey
Thomas Wm. Hunter
Charles W. Lister
Wm. F. Lofthouse (*P.*, 1929)
Albert E. Nightingale
Wilfrid B. Trewhella
George Whitley
George E. Woodford

1896
Walter J. Ashton
William H. Barden
Charles Borman
Edgar J. Bradford
Thomas H. Caddy
Enoch Carter
Harry R. Crosby
Dingley P. Fuge
Arthur A. Fuller
T. Hamilton Groves
Georges Guilliame
Robert H. Gush
Herbert W. Hamon
Stanley N. Hoare
Llewellyn Morgan
William Hy. Phipps
C. Clouston Porri
Ernest Pratt
T. Glyn Roberts
Lorenzo S. H. Wilkinson
Fredk. J. Williams

1897
H. Osborne Arnett
Frederick J. Bomford

1897—cont.

Ernest C. Cooper
Edward Geo. Edmonds
William W. Gibson
Joshua Hoyle
Frederick A. Lees
E. E. Ley Peake
J. Duncan Percy
Frederick J. Pope
Richard T. Richards
William Rider
John Henry Roberts
J. Marwood Sanderson
George Sara
Henry Scott
Edward Smith
Richard R. Tregunna
Ernest W. Trounson
Harry W. Wade
Arthur H. Wilks
Richard H. Wray

1898

Moïse Alain
G. Gower Cocks
William J. Holford
R. Wilson Hopkins
Ernest J. Jones
Benjamin Lowe
T. Major
Edward Frank Piper
Arthur J. Revnell
Harold Spencer
Wm. J. Tunbridge
A. F. Parkinson Turnbull
Arthur Walters
Eric S. Waterhouse

1899

Henry P. Atkins
Walter J. Bull
Charles Escritt
Wm. E. Garman
Edward Gearey
Henry G. Godwin
Francis J. Gould
Francis G. Gray
James T. Harris
J. Sidney Helps
Sidney R. Hicks
Walter James
W. A. Bryan Jones
George P. Lester
Ernest V. Paget
Joseph E. Reeves
Charles H. S. Ward
W. Morley P. Wilkes

1900

Jabez Robert Ackroyd
Herbert J. Baker
George S. Barber
Frank C. Beecher
Wilfred H. Boocock
P. Middleton Brumwell
H. Jones Davies
Arthur Edmunds
John M. Hughes
T. Faulkner Jefferis
John J. Johnston
William Pillow
Edward R. Polsom
Joseph H. E. Smith
Edwin A. Spear
George Walker
James Walton
Harry Webster
Frank W. Wilkes
Percy M. Wright

1901

Charles H. Beagley
Wesley T. Bosward
Herbert M. Brown
G. Percy Gibbens
Wm. T. Grantham
Wilfrid L. Hannam
Frank Hart

RICHMOND COLLEGE

William Henderson
Reginald J. P. Julian
Holmes Keall
T. Maltby Kerruish
Ernest G. Loosley
Arthur S. Lyne
Thomas Oliver
Peter Humphrey Pierce
F. Dyson Winston

1902

W. Routley Bailey
Alfred J. Bromwich
Philip S. Burrow
Charles J. Cumberworth
Ernest Frith
Arthur Sydney Hunt
S. W. M. Ingersent
Edgar Jackson
Vincent Johnson
T. Llewellyn Jones
Roderick M. Kedward
Arthur W. Keeley
T. Fredk. Lewis
C. Claud Mayes
John Mullineux
Wm. Stanley Osborne
John E. Reilly
Anthony T. Skyrme
William Solomon
Owen R. Thompson
George A. Vernon
James Webster
J. Howard Weir
R. Twiston Williams

1903

John Wm. Almond
Robert Coutts
Wm. Edw. Cullwick
Shirley B. Cumberland
Henry W. Edwards
Atrhur F. G. Fletcher
Richard Francis
Francis G. Gatehouse

Ira G. Goldhawk
John W. Hallam
Arthur T. Jubb
W. Killick
A. W. Glasson
R. Gibson Lawn
T. Harold Mallinson
Ernest Marshall
Frank Masters
W. Arthur Moore
Edward Owen
Allen F. Parsons
Hugh A. Roberts
J. Scarabin
E. Hardy Scott
Arthur R. Slater
Fred. W. Vaughan
W. Warmington

1904

O. Gordon Bolton
Arthur E. Boyce
Arthur K. Brown
Geo. S. Burden
W. Clifford Caddy
Percy T. Cash
Harry Chellew
John D. Coutts
L. S. Creed
A. Garfield Curnow
Ernest Dennis
Alfred T. Fakeley
Henry J. Foss
John E. Howard
L. M. Larrington
Wesley J. Parry
Charles Pengelly
Wm. Proctor
Wm. M. Rapson
Matthew Rodda
Wm. Rosewarne
William G. Salmon
H. W. Stanton
Tom Stephenson
Harry Taylor
Paul Wood

1905

Reginald W. Baker
Hy. Jas. Barber
A. Percy Bourne
Alfred Geo. Burnham
Geo. J. Chamberlain
Wm. Lamplough Doughty
Wilfrid E. Garment
F. Percy Gent
G. Osborn Gregory
J. Fisher Griffiths
Joseph A. Handley
Francis C. Hoggarth
Arthur J. Jeffries
C. Deane Little
Arch. J. Marchant
H. Arthur Meek
Norman V. Moore
Fredk. J. Paine
T. R. J. Phillips
Ernest P. Raithby
D. Rowlands Rowe
J. Opie Urmson
William H. Warren
Edward Wyman

1906

T. Christmas Anwyl
J. Edward Dark
Ernest E. Dewing
Chas. H. Hodgson
Frederick Hudson
Alfred Knottenbelt
E. Owen Lane
Donald Macmillan
Arthur E. Parkes
Herbert Pearson
Louis P. Porri
Eric Robertson
J. Harold Robinson
Leonard Sainsbury
Wm. W. Shilling
T. Jasper Shovel
A. Hanley Smith
Thomas Tiplady

Benjamin A. Trew
Walter W. Vicary
Richard A. Wilkinson
G. Arthur Wooding

1907

Charles Fredk. Brend
Edmund G. H. Bryant
Frederick T. Buckingham
Arthur M. Chirgwin
Wm. Crossley
A. Birkett Duncalfe
Frederick P. Evans
Francis S. Foss
Herbert J. Franklin
G. Kellett Grice
James T. Hudson
A. Price Hughes
Aubrey White Ingram
A. Gordon James
Leslie V. Jolly
Albert G. Kick
Josiah D. Martin
G. Eric Mees
Robert H. Pritchard
H. Owen Roberts
Vincent Taylor
Edward John Thompson
W. Edgar Wallis
H. Crawford Walters
Wm. T. Whalley
L. Rowell Winter

1908

Richard Ladd Canney
A. Evans Clarke
George Conning
John Elias Davies
J. Wilson Ferry
R. Everett Jayne
W. Arthur Kirkman
C. Treverrow Lander
Ebenezer Leonard
Percy C. Mellor

RICHMOND COLLEGE

Robert E. Newton
J. Richard Roberts
Thomas A. Roberts
G. Cloudesley Shovel
J. T. Fredk. Smith
Frank Spencer
Raynor Speight
Eardley B. Stringer
Donald Stuart
William Sunter
Albion J. Trebilco
Herbert J. West
Geo. Hy. Dyer Wright

Robt. H. Hingley
Joseph T. Hodgson
William G. Hughes
C. Edgar James
Thomas.W. Kingsnorth
John Wesley Lewis
Roland F. Priestley
William Sawkins
G. Jarvis Smith
G. Samuel Smith
Chris. H. Tice
W. Robinson Turner
J. Mervyn Young

1909

Robert Armstrong
Horace E. Atkins
W. Jas. Beckett
Holman Brown
F. Norman Charley
Benjamin A. Gregory
Cecil T. Groves
Harry A. Hindle
Sydney P. Jacoby
Ivor T. Kempster
M. Herbert Lee
J. Ernest Matthews
J. Hopkin Morgan
John Pickles
Maurice H. Russell
Arthur E. Southon
H. Bemrose Spencer
H. Donald Spencer
T. L. Barlow Westerdale
C. Bowers Wildblood
Chas. J. Wright

1910

Percy E. Beale
Norman E. Dando
William H. Dimmock
Albert J. Farnsworth
J. Lewis Gillians
Frederick W. Henley

1911

W. Siberton Baker
Stanley H. Bosward
Joseph Coombes
C. Gordon Early
Harold G. Fiddick
Douglas E. Field
George Gifford
Reginald J. H. Hill
Peter T. Hutchison
David Lewis Jones
T. Bernard Jones
Samuel Magor
Thomas Martin
Ernest P. Picken
Richard A. Rees
Joseph A. Robertson
Ivan D. Ross
Fredk. W. Shaw
Granville S. Smith
Harold W. Stephenson
H. Herbert Symmons
Samuel Thomas
Adolphus N. Walker

1912

Bert Adcock
Geo. W. Alway
T. Stanley Cannon
Leslie H. Clench

1912—cont.

Leonard W. Dickens
Herbert Green
Fred. A. Hickling
Llewellyn Kendrick
James Mullineux
W. James Neal
William A. Parrott
Herbert Phelps
J. Herbert Price
Robert T. Roberts
Alan Roughley
Joseph R. Rushton
Ernest Smith
H. Stanley Southall
Alec. R. Spooner
W. Edmund Thomas
H. Owen Wagstaff
J. A. Colston Copston
Joseph Williams

T. Kenneth Barnsley
Basil B. Burnett
Frank T. Copplestone
Arthur B. Geden
W. Elmslie Hawkins
H. John Ivens
Chas. Robt. Keene
G. Hadlett Kingswood
H. G. Leverton
William J. Lewis
Ernest H. Livesley
Sidney F. Lunn
A. Denman Martin
Ernest F. Pawson
A. Gordon Read
J. H. Reed
Frank W. Spencer
Arthur G. Utton
Geo. N. Waights
Geo. H. Wayne

1913

Arthur B. Cannon
Wm. T. Croxford
John M. Darlington
J. Rees Davies
Bertram Dewhirst
Henry R. Hindley
Edmund C. Horler
T. Jones Hughes
John Leale
Frank W. Ross
Stanley P. Rundle
Fredk. A. Thomas
Fredk. W. Townsend
T. Arthur Udy
Leslie D. Weatherhead
E. Carvan Young

1914

A. Edward Banks
C. Rowley Barker

1915

Eric S. Allwood[1]
Wm. G. Baldwin[1]
E. Mervyn Blow
Hy. Geo. Campbell
Robt. G. Hughes
Leonard W. Juby[1]
John Proctor Lund
Raymond C. Mace
Ernest May
Ernest C. Raynes
Walter T. Rose
Alfred Salmon[1]
Arthur Simmons

1920

Harold J. Allner
John Ashton
Thomas H. Baker
Alexander C. Blain

[1] Re-entered 1920.

RICHMOND COLLEGE 183

David J. Bowen
A. Bernard Brockway
Harold Buxton
Harold Champion
A. Reginald Cole
Jas. R. Course
Jas. H. Cox
W. Talbot Ellams
Robert Flenley
Thomas R. Foulger
Walter Geo. Fowles
D. Marson Frost
Charles A. Getliff
Sydney J. Granville
Joseph Frederick S. Hall
Philip Hall
William Horner
George Jenkins
Gilbert E. Jessop
Lionel H. Jones
W. George Jones
Karl R. Kitt
Ernest H. Lawrence
Herbert R. Matthews
Chas. McCarthy
J. Clifford Mitchell
D. Arthur Morgan
Clifford H. Osborne
B. Hedd Owen
Ephraim J. Pike
Albert V. L. Powell
Harold T. Procter
Jas. Rees
Frank B. Roberts
J. Osborne Roberts
Eugene B. Robin
Philip Romeril
W. Edwin Sangster
Jas. W. Sawyer
H. Vincent Shepherd
Albert Jas. Short
M. Roy Smith
Fredk. Edward Stacey
Edgar F. Thomas
A. Reginald Todd
Rhys Thomas Williams
Malcolm Womack

1921

Henry G. Arnold
Cyril G. Baker
Harry J. Basham
Reginald Chaloner
E. Lynn Cragg
Harold W. Goldsack
Ernest Higman
Norman W. Harrison
Sydney G. Janney
D. Paget Main
John G. Morton
Bernard R. K. Paintin
James Paulson
Henry S. F. Rossiter
H. W. Kenneth Sandy
John Vivian Thomas
J. Leslie Webb

1922

Percy E. Bannister
E. Stanley Cheeseright
H. Hector Chick
Arthur Powell Davies
J. Frank Froud
Reginald Glanville
J. Ernest Griffin
Harry Johnson
Giacomo A. Lardi
A. Kingsley Lloyd
Percy C. Oliff
Hugh W. Price
Lionel J. Sheasby
E. Oliver Sutton
Wesley F. Swift
Clarence Thorpe
John A. Wells

1923

Jas. S. Boulton
Edgar H. Bowen
Cecil H. G. Carter
Roland L. Cox
Wesley J. Culshaw

1923—cont.

Thos. E. Deakin
Wm. J. D. Evans
G. Eric Firth
Ernest H. Hardy
John Hunt
Alfred T. Johns
Walter Pollard
Wm. Chas. Roberts
A. Walter Selby
Cecil H. Sheasby
Charles A. Somerscales
Reg. R. Stallard
John T. Webb

1924

L. T. Marsden Allen
William J. Barrett
Joseph I. Brice
Cyrus Burge
Kenneth H. Crosby
Anson E. F. Garrett
Norman Glanville
W. Russell Hall
Charles Jewell
E. Redvers Jones
Gerald Lansley
Frederick E. Lines
Leslie A. Newman
Cyril C. Payne
Norman H. Pike
H. Cecil Pomroy
Roland W. Roberts
Leo. E. Sanders
Stanley Victor Sheasby
Rudland Showell
Henry Sturdy
Erris C. H. Tribbeck
J. Hollis Walker
R. Leslie Waterman
Joseph N. Williams

1925

Henry A. H. Arnett
Windsor Bevan
Fredk. E. Christmas
C. Horace F. Cory
G. Kenneth Eustice
W. Davis Evans
Edward A. Flowerday
H. Maurice Hart
Harold Wm. Hindsley
Leslie N. Holden
Laurence D. Jefferd
J. Rodney McNeal
Stewart H. Moody
Arthur G. Payne
W. Arnold Pendlebury
Herbert E. C. Pettet
William T. Price
John H. Robinson
Fernand Rodet
Arthur Whitmore
Wm. Winchurch

1926

J. Harold Armstrong
E. A. Philip Attwater
Harold A. Bishop
Reginald J. Brown
W. Cyril Cardy
Leslie T. D. Chapman
Hugh G. Collins
Raymond Cook
Arthur R. Cornwall
G. Henry Dunford
Ernest W. Eavis
E. David Edwards
Wilfred Guy
Leonard Harrison
Horace G. L. Hinchcliffe
John H. Humphreys
Harold Key
J. Oswald Law
E. Rowton Lee
Bernard Lewis
Thomas Metcalf
Arthur D. Moore
William J. R. Nash
Denis Reed
Sydney Sargeant

RICHMOND COLLEGE

Thos. H. Sprague
Clifford K. Storey
Geo. G. Trevithick

1927

Walter Brown
Maurice A. Clarke
Frank Cumbers
Hubert F. Daniels
Wilfred Easton
Geo. Wm. Gill
Harold A. Guy
David N. Heap
Helier J. Herivel
Arthur S. Howarth
Wilfred H. Hulbert
William S. Liddle
Wilfrid McKee
George M. Russell
John W. J. Scott
E. Quintin Snook
John Wm. Timms
John W. Thomson
W. Morley Waite
T. Harry Wakeford
Eric M. Walker
Alfred Waterhouse
Raymond B. Wright

1928

Joseph Allistoun
Edward Avery
Kenneth G. Bloxham
Reginald T. Bowles
Herbert J. Crocker
R. James Day
R. Harvey Field
William R. Gilbert
Leslie Hall
Arthur Hoyles
Joseph N. Jory
Frank H. Longley
G. Robinson Myers
R. W. Debenham Peck

Cyril J. Phillips
Thomas Russell
Charles T. Staden
Douglas C. Thompson
Ernest B. Wright

1929

E. Tomlin Barton
Harry J. Blackmore
Arthur R. Burch
Allan H. Carter
Alfred Cartwright
J. Henry Clay
Francis H. Coles
N. Tasker Colley
Malcolm E. Dixon
J. Bonney Eade
Stephen Frith
Richard Hailwood
David M. Jones
Tecwyn Jones
Ralph Kirby
Sidney W. Lipscomb
Richard A. Marsh
Hubert J. Martin
E. Howard Metherell
E. Geoffrey Parrinder
Robert W. Pridmore
D. Maldwyn Rowlands
Eric R. Sarchet
Ernest Sawyer
Russell B. Spear
Albert J. Stanbury
J. Wesley Webb
Edgar T. Wood

1930

Hedley C. Browning
J. Govett Caunter
George C. Cotterell
Thomas J. Foinette
John N. Foster
Ernest W. Funnell

1930—cont.

George J. Gage
T. Francis Glasson
Karl A. Gray
Goronwy Jones-Davies
J. Victor Josey
Edward J. Le Poidevin
D. Albert Lewis
Geoffrey N. Stephens
Leslie M. Thompson
W. J. Ronald Tucker
Frank A. White

1931

Victor Burns
Eric G. Chapman
Leslie G. Farmer
Eric G. Frost
Otto Glombitza
Joseph Heaven
E. Kingsley Hodson
K. Vaughan Jones
Lawrence Linton
R. Hubert Luke
Norman M. Robinson
Yannick Scarabin
Percy Scott
George H. Sully
John Wilson

1932

Richard A. W. Boggis
Harry Charleston
Levi Dawson
Atherton Didier
Thomas F. Fenton
Stanley B. Frost
Reginald L. George
Norman Greenhalgh
Frank W. Hargreaves
Arthur J. Hichens
Leslie G. Holding
Kenneth J. Holt
Arnold B. Jones
R. Lloyd Jones
Douglas Lansley
George Lawton
George H. Maskell
Erich Pongs
John R. Sharp
T. Leslie Thexton
Kenneth E. Woodruff
John Wright

1933

Edwin W. A. Barber
Henry J. Christian
W. Ivor Claydon
William C. Dyer
S. Austen Eddy
John Hy. Fisher
H. Bramwell Howard
Kenneth E. Jinks
Kenneth Johnson
Owen R. Johnson
Reginald Kissack
Albert C. Mortlock
David Pike
Andre Roux
Carus L. Trevenna
Howard A. Trevis
Rudolf Weckerling
Leonard E. White

1934

Reginald W. Hopper
A. Gordon Jones
Percy W. Mably
P. Stewart May
George B. Middleton
T. Trevor Parry
Edgar Richards
George Richards
Eric L. Robinson
Maldwyn O. Williams

RICHMOND COLLEGE 187

1935
Howard A. G. Belben
Anthony S. Chadwick
Philip J. Child
Allan H. Currey
Peredur W. Jones
Keith M. Keeley
William G. Marchant
Norman M. Slaughter
H. Richmond Stuart

1936
Harry Allen
Wm. C. Dowling
Eddie Greetham
Eric Gulliford
John Millns
P. Napier Milne
Francis Meuret
Rowland F. Newland
Thos. H. Norman
Roy Livingstone Pitkin
Enno Reichel
Edward T. Scott
Frank T. Squire
S. Clive Thexton
Arthur S. Yates

1937
Kenneth S. Armitstead
Richard Cullington
Roy Delbridge
Raymond M. Goodall
J. Bartlett Healey
Percival A. J. Hill
Maurice W. Kirk
John Mellor
W. Peter D. Morley
Kenneth J. Payne
Max Scheid
Joseph O. E. Soremekun

Thos. H. Wood
E. Burton Wright

1938
Stanley A. Barrass
Hans Bolewski
Leslie G. Buckingham
Norman Carter
Francis Henry Case
Oliver M. Darwin
G. Herber Davies
Alan B. Dawson
Sidney C. Fittall
Edward G. Green
H. Stanley Hills
Ronald A. Jefferies
Matthew Lassey
W. Eric Mantle
Robert W. Pile
B. Arthur Shaw
Trevor J. Smith
Francis R. Street
Walter Suffield
Alfred E. Taylor
Kenneth Underwood

1939
Thomas P. Addison
Ernest A. Ball
André E. S. Beach
Wyndham E. Bold
Harry Button
Norman N. G. Cope
Arthur J. Fielder
Maurice D. Gatehouse
Eryl W. Hughes
A. E. Glendower Jones
Richard Keen
Wm. Joseph Martyn
John Morgan
W. Maurice Nicholas
T. Tanimowo Solaru
Hugh W. Tattersall

1939—cont.

Merfyn M. Temple
T. Torkington Williams
Eilhard Zichgraf

1940

Anthony S. Bennett
Fredk. Wm. Bliss
G. Thompson Brake
Leonard D. Brenton
Frank Brice
Frederick W. Clifford
D. Claude Hearle
A. Walter Hiscox
J. Frederick Jones (B)
Walter J. Joyce
Geoffrey Joycey
Robert Lewis
Donald H. Mason
Wesley U. Penney
C. Elwyn Perry
Lawrence Proctor
Austin J. Rees
W. Allan Shaw
Wm. Strawson
Raymond Warner

INDEX

ALAIN, MOISE, 145

BARBER, W. T. A., 92, 116
Barratt, T. H., 84, 115
Barrett, Alfred, 102
Barton, E. C., 140
Bateson, J. H., 136
Beet, J. Agar, 70, 74, 79, 110, 132
Bestall, A. H., 136
Bisseker, Harry, 84, 116
Bottrill, Edwin, 144
Bradford, E. J., 141
Briscoe, F. J., 144
Brixton, Mr., 44
Brown, J. Milton, 132
Brumwell, P. Middleton, 141
Brunyate, Wesley, 129
Burnet, Amos, 135

CADMAN, S. PARKES, 137
Calvert, James, 128
Cape, A. Trevellick, 140
Cape, C. Phillips, 140
Cawood, Wm. B., 144
Church, L. F., 120
Clogg, F. B., 96, 119
Cocks, G. Gower, 141
Cornaby, W. A., 136

DALLINGER, W. H., 131
Darrell, J. H., 140
Davison, W. T., 64, 69, 83, 95, 109
Dimond, S. G., 121
Dyson, W. H., 96

EARLY, GORDON, 82
Elliott, J. A., 136
Eva, G. H., 144

FARRAR, JOHN, 100
Faure, Auguste, 145
Fiddick, Harold G., 142
Findlay, G. G., 108, 134
Findlay, W. G., 120
Findlay, W. H., 135
Fittall, S. C., 49
Fletcher, George, 74, 79, 95, 112, 129

GARRETT, CHARLES, 129
Gathercole, J. H., 145
Gautrey, Moffatt, 140
Geden, A. S., 75, 80, 83, 113
Geden, J. B., 128
Gibson, W. W., 141
Goldhawk, Ira, 142
Goudie, James, 136
Goudie, William, 135
Gregory, G. Osborn, 142
Grice, G. Kellett, 123
Griffin, Oliver J., 140
Griffiths, David, 22

HAIGH, HENRY, 134
Hannam, W. L., 146
Hartley, Marshall, 134
Harvard, W. M., 101
Hellier, Benjamin, 101, 128
Helps, J. S., 141
Highfield, H. G., 129
Hill, David, 131
Holdsworth, W. W., 136
Hudson, J., 131
Hughes, H. Price, 23, 76, 132, 153
Humphrey, William, 140
Hunt, J., 128

INGRAM, R., 74
Ives, E. J., 145

JACKSON, GEORGE, 137
Jackson, Samuel, 101
Jackson, Thomas, 100
James, A. Gordon, 143
James, Walter, 141
Jones, D. M., 151

KELLETT, F. W., 68, 122

LAMPLOUGH, MR. E. S., 46
Letcher, O. J., 140
Lofthouse, W. F., 140
Lomas, John, 103
Lord, J. W., 135

MEE, JOSIAH, 134
Moreton, R. H., 132

INDEX

Morton, Harold C., 138
Monahan, C. H., 138
Moulton, W. F., 106

NAPIER, F. P., 108
Nicholson, Edward, 137
North, C. R., 120

OSBORN, GEORGE, 66, 104

PILLOW, W. H., 141
Pope, F. J., 141
Pope, W. B., 128
Posnett, C. W., 138
Posnett, J., 129
Punshon, W. M., 128

REILLY, J. E., 142
Restarick, A. E., 136
Revnell, A. J., 141
Ritson, J. H., 46
Roberts, Harold, 121
Robins, Mr. F., 57, 151

SANDERSON, DANIEL, 69, 105
Sangster, W. E., 93, 143
Sara, George, 141
Scarabin, Jean, 142
Sharp, J. A., 48
Sharpley, A. E., 117
Shimmin, I., 44a, 132
Skinner, Conrad, 84, 96
Smith, C. Ryder, 91, 117

Solomon, S. R. B., 137
Southall, H. Stanley, 143
Southon, A. E., 143
Stamp, W. W., 101
Stephenson, Bowman, 129
Stephenson, Thos., 75

TASKER, J. G., 69, 111, 135
Taylor, T. M., 137
Taylor, Vincent, 142
Thompson, E. W., 140
Thompson, Edward, 143
Tiplady, Thos., 142
Titcomb, Ernest, 145
Turner, Philip C., 101

UNDERWOOD, K., 148

VANES, J. A., 114

WALLER, A. J., 129
Walters, C. E., 138
Waterhouse, E. S., 92, 118, 141
Watkins, Owen, 132
Watkins, Owen Spencer, 139
Watkinson, W. L., 129
Wayte, J. H., 22
Weatherhead, L. D., 143
Weavind, G., 144
Wiseman, Luke H., 128
Wright, C. J., 143

YOUNG, E. CARVAN, 143
Young, R. Newton, 129

www.ingramcontent.com/pod-product-compliance
Lightning Source LLC
Chambersburg PA
CBHW062043220426
43662CB00010B/1624